"Five parts Socrates to three parts David Hume to two parts *Calvin & Hobbes*, Lyonhart provides ordinary lay readers with a disarmingly sophisticated account of the Trinity, the church, free will, faith, morality, love, and, as Douglas Adams might have put it, "life, the universe, and everything." *MonoThreeism* may well be absurdly arrogant, but it is also enormously useful, as well as being a good deal of fun. I can hardly wait to recommend it to my students."

—**CRAIG GAY**
Author of *Modern Technology and the Human Future*

"MonoThreeism is truly a masterful work that entertains the academy, engages the skeptic, and edifies the church. Let J. D. Lyonhart take you on a journey from the lowest small talk in a bar, to the highest concepts of heaven, to the emotional depths of the soul."

—**SY HUFFER**
Lead pastor, College Heights Christian Church, Joplin, Missouri

"This fascinating book is the welcome attempt of a fearless young theologian to make the reality of God the Holy Trinity accessible and relevant at a popular level. If God is truly Trinity, and if there is no God 'back of' the three divine persons in coinherent communion, who share the divine essence and are equal in honor, and if knowing Jesus by the Spirit means knowing the Father, and if the triune being of God is more than a doctrine but a way of seeing the world and the cosmos, and if the Trinity is truly the center and architectonic of theology and life, then the message of this book is worthwhile, indeed vital, for all humanity. It is both entertaining and enlightening."

—**ROSS HASTINGS**
Regent College

"Truly groundbreaking. Lyonhart has put the fundamental meaning of Trinitarian theology into a cohesive package that should be useful to interested skeptics as well as dedicated believers. It perfectly illustrates and illuminates the complexities of the Trinity as well as the Trinity's impact on all of our lives."

—**CODY GRAVES**
Lead pastor, First Christian Church, Baxter Springs, Kansas

MonoThreeism

MONOTHREEISM

An Absurdly Arrogant Attempt to Answer
All the Problems of the Last 2000 Years
in One Night at a Pub

JD Lyonhart

CASCADE *Books* · Eugene, Oregon

MONOTHREEISM
An Absurdly Arrogant Attempt to Answer All the Problems of the Last 2000 Years in One Night at a Pub

Cascade Books
An Imprint of Wipf and Stock Publishers
199 W. 8th Ave., Suite 3
Eugene, OR 97401

www.wipfandstock.com

PAPERBACK ISBN: 978-1-7252-6268-3
HARDCOVER ISBN: 978-1-7252-6267-6
EBOOK ISBN: 978-1-7252-6269-0

Cataloguing-in-Publication data:

Names: Lyonhart, JD. (Jonathan David), author

Title: Monothreeism : an absurdly arrogant attempt to answer all the problems of the last 2000 years in one night at a pub / JD Lyonhart.

Description: Eugene, OR: Cascade Books 2021 | Includes bibliographical references.

Identifiers: ISBN 978-1-7252-6268-3 (paperback) | ISBN 978-1-7252-6267-6 (hardcover) | ISBN 978-1-7252-6269-0 (ebook)

Subjects: LCSH: Trinity | Trinity—Criticism, interpretation, etc. | Apologetics | Metaphysics | Christian Theology | God (Christianity) | Philosophical theology | Religion—Philosophy | Triads (Philosophy)

Classification: BT111.3 L96 2021 (paperback) | BT111.3 (ebook)

Manufactured in the U.S.A.   06/29/21

To my sons

Contents

Acknowledgments

TOO MANY PEOPLE HAVE helped me along the way to thank everyone. But as a start, I would like to thank: My wife, Madison, whose willingness to endure my rants and indulge my nomadic mind has enabled this odd little book to arrive. My mother, who read through numerous drafts. Seth, for arguing with me for years about this idea. Art and Jenny, for listening patiently while I rabbit-trailed through early, unrefined versions of the project (and for just being amazing in general). Tom, for his valuable feedback on the manuscript, as well as his invaluable friendship. VCLC, who gave me the support and confidence to pull this off. Brian, whose encouragement prevented me waiting another twenty years before daring to put pen to paper. Andrew, who spent hours discussing square-triangles with me, planting the seed that grew into this book. Mark, whose fatherly affirmation of this idea back in 2009 gave me the self-assurance to keep going. Craig, for giving me permission to read, write, and run loose on this project. Sy, Cody, Atlas, Peter, Adam, Cooper, and Matt, who each spent hours consulting on the manuscript.

I

THE TWO

Idi: Vlad!! . . . Vlad, you big idiot, *I'm over here!*

> *Vlad weaves in and out of pub tables toward Idi, knocking the occasional shoulder. As Vlad nears, he sees a copy of David Hume's* Dialogues concerning Natural Religion *lying open in Idi's lap.*

Vlad: I already know where you are. You're where we sit *every single week.*

Idi: I know. I just like yelling.

Vlad: *I know.* I just like giving you a hard time.

Idi: Sit. Drink. . . . Barkeep!

Vlad: You don't have to yell at her.

Idi: See my previous statement.

> *The bartender, Mira, slides down the bar to greet them.*

Mira: What'll it be professors?

Idi: Two vodkas!

Vlad: One vodka. I will be having a diet coke.

Idi: No!!

Vlad: Yes. I've got stuff in the morning.

Idi: No you don't! It's Christmas Eve!

Vlad: Exactly. *It's Christmas Eve.*

Idi: No!

Vlad: Yes.

Idi: No.

Vlad: Yes.

Idi: Nein!

Vlad: Ja.

Idi: Nett.

Vlad: Da.

Idi: Minime!

Vlad: Mini-me?

Idi: It's Latin for "not at all." Its where we get "minimal" from.

Vlad: Interesting.

Mira: . . . As adorable as I'm sure you think this is . . .

Vlad: Sorry. A diet coke for me and an IV drip for him. Just leave the needle, he knows what to do with it.

Idi: I do. I really do.

Mira: I'll come back.

Idi: No!

Vlad: And she's gone. . . . . Here, enjoy this delightfully festive bowl of nuts and candy canes.

Idi: You're mocking me.

Vlad: Yes, but out of love. You're in dire need of Christmas mockery. What's your sermon on tomorrow at university chapel?

Idi: Guess!

Vlad: Just tell me.

Idi: It's the same bloody Christmas sermon I repackage every year. I don't have time between classes to prep something new.

Vlad: Then why did you agree to do it when I asked?

Idi: Things were different then. So much has happened since.

Vlad: It was yesterday.

Idi: Yes, but you see, I've recently decided it's all stupid.

Vlad: Oh, when did that happen?

Idi: A few minutes ago. Well, no, it started when I was ten, but it's been happening on and off ever since.

Vlad: Of course. What's it this time?

Idi: It's *everything.* It's God and doubt and church and all that gooey nonsense. It's the cumulative weight of ridiculousness piled upon preposterousness like pancakes.

Vlad: There's a line between alliterating and illiterate and you're flirting with it.

Idi: The first of my woes . . .

Vlad: Here we go.

Idi: . . . is the Trinity. The beatific bodice itself. The mathematical marvel; the only time it is ever okay to tell children that one plus one plus one equals . . . wait for it . . . one! One God, three persons. Three and one, one and three, n' such.

Vlad: So just the whole *God* part of your religion then?

Idi: Yep! Somehow the Father is God, the Son is God, and the Spirit is God, yet you're supposed to believe there is only one God. It makes *no* sense. At chapel you ask me to lead people in the liturgy once a month, and each time I stand up there wondering if I still really believe in this Father, Son, and Holy Ghost. As we used to snicker under our breath in school: "Our Father, who fart in heaven."

Vlad: Forgive him Father, for he knows exactly what he does.

Idi: The second of my woes . . .

Vlad: Ah, there's more.

Idi: . . . is the incarnation.

Vlad: Speaking of *carne,* could you please get us carnivores some barbecue wings, Mira?

Mira: And to drink?

Vlad: I think we need another minute. He's monologuing.

Idi: . . . My second objection! . . . is the incarnation. How can Jesus be 100 percent God, but also 100 percent Middle Eastern man-flesh? Truly human and truly divine, in heaven and on earth, up there and down here? How can the all-mighty maker of everything become a baby who whines, suckles, and defecates? How can the eternal grow up? How can the Prime Mover go through puberty! Think about it: God had pimples! Probably great big volcano whiteheads! He was probably an awkward Jewish kid who wasn't good at sports. And then to top it off, this eternal being gets what? Killed. The holy gets hammered! The one who was, and is, and is to come, ceases to be. How's that logic for you? The incarnation is a contradiction of the highest order. The manger is empty. Christmas is a crock.

Vlad: I know you're not drunk yet. You don't have to play the part.

Idi: My third woe! . . .

> *A long pause follows.*

Vlad: Yes?

Idi: I was waiting for you to make a snide remark.

Vlad: Your mother smells of Elderbe—

Idi: —My third woe! . . . is that religion is so busy with heaven it forgets about earth. Religion doesn't like the body, flesh, pleasure, or sex, and makes you feel guilty if you do. All that matters is dying and going to heaven. Religion trades the physical for the spiritual, the real for the invisible, the "now" for some future in the clouds that may never come. You know that song? *"Imagine there's no heaven, . . . it's eas—"*

Vlad: —I know the song. Everyone in the world knows the song. *Please stop singing the song.*

Idi: Fine. But only because it's time for my next objection: Free will! It doesn't make any sense. If we are just a collection of atoms bouncing around like cogs in a machine, then how do we have any freedom?

Vlad: There are views of free will that are compatible with atoms and determinism and all that.

Idi: Ya, but those views are stupid.

Vlad: No they aren't.

Idi: Sorry, what I meant was that the people who believe in those views are stupid.

Vlad: . . .

Idi: Just think about it. All our choices are caused by a long link of causes that extends back before we were even born. I chose this path because my daddy did this, because his daddy did that, because the class system is oppressive and Napoleon was short. Everything we do has a cause, and if you follow the causes they go back way before us, so they weren't really our choices at all. Therefore! free will is bogus, in which case all that religious guilt about whether or not you choose to have premarital sex—or abort your baby after said sex—is bogus too. You can't fault me for getting absolutely piss drunk tonight, because I didn't have any choice.

Vlad: And you can't fault me for leaving you here in your own puke.

Idi: Agreed. Now, for my fifth woe . . . I shall whine about . . . *the soul*!!

Vlad: Are you upset you didn't get one?

Idi: Silence heathen! Now, do humans have a soul? If so, then why has neuroscience advanced so far while describing the brain in entirely material terms? And even if we did have a soul, how could it relate to our body? If the body is material and the soul is immaterial, then how can they interact? It would be like Casper the friendly ghost trying to kiss a human girl. She'd just slip through his fingers.

Vlad: Are you almost done?

Idi: We're not even in double digits yet. My sixth woe . . . drumroll please . . . is . . . *the problem of evil!* If free will is bogus then you can't really say it's humanity's fault for mucking up the cosmos, because we didn't have any say in the matter. Hitler couldn't have done otherwise; its Gods fault for creating him that way and making him bad at art . . .

Idi pauses for breath and for dramatic effect.

Idi: Thus, God is responsible for all the anger and abuse and bad fathers. For all the imperialism, slaves, crusades, witch-hunts, wars, gulags, gas, and ghettos.

Vlad: So just all the problems of the last few thousand years then?

Idi: Furthermore! What about all the other religions? The Muslims have Allah, the Greeks have the pantheon, and the Hindus have . . . whatever it is that they have.

Vlad rolls his eyes.

Idi: So even if you could make sense of the Trinity, why is that conception of God better than all the others? And! How can people be faulted for being born outside a Christian country and never having the chance to choose Jesus in the first place!

Vlad: Which wouldn't matter anyway because choice is an illusion?

Idi: Precisely! Have a peanut.

Idi pushes the bar nuts over to Vlad. The usual nuts have been re-placed by candy canes for the Christmas season, but the flakey remnants of ancient almonds still linger at the bottom. Vlad's nose flairs up in disgust, then he remembers the candy canes are in protective wrappers, helping himself to one.

Idi: For my ninth woe! . . . I will—

Vlad: —eighth.

Idi: What?

Vlad: You skipped one. You're only on eight.

Idi: No I didn't, the other religions thing was implicitly its own woe.

Vlad: I know, I counted it. Even with it you're only on eight.

Idi: For my eighth woe! I will summon Sigmund Schlomo Freud!

Vlad: Schlomo?

Idi: Sigmund *Schlomo* Freud showed that God is just a projection of us. Daddy didn't love us, so we invented a bearded father in the clouds to give us all the affection we need. We took human attributes, magnified them in our heads, and subconsciously projected them onto the clouds. Everything man is in small measure God is in big measure. Humans know some things; God knows everything. Man likes power; God is all-powerful. We just take what humans are in finite measure, multiply that by a bunch, and get an infinite God. God is just a projection of ourselves. *Theology is anthropology.*

Vlad: That was Feuerbach.

Idi: What?

Vlad: Theology is anthropology. That's a quote from Feuerbach, not Freud.

Idi: Stop interrupting.

Vlad: Stop meriting interru—

Idi: —Nine! This objection is the opposite of the last. If the last one said God is too human and so is just a projection of us, then this objection says the opposite. If God is supposed to be this eternal, infinite, mysterious, transcendent, wholly Other being off in the clouds, then how can we even talk about him? How can language contain him? And that's the problem; if God fits into our human categories then he is just a projection of us. But if he doesn't fit into our categories then he is too "Other" for us to talk about at all. Damned if you do, damned if you don't.

> *Idi pauses just long enough for Vlad to begin to open his mouth to speak, before thundering in again.*

Idi: Ten! There is no meaning—

Vlad: —Mira, I'm gonna need some gin.

Mira: And tonic?

Vlad: No. Just straight gin. And some earplugs if you have them.

Idi: Number ten!! There is no objective meaning or morality in the universe. We can say what is culturally good at one time for one group of people, but we cannot transcend our context to reach some sort of metaphysical declaration about what is absolutely good at all times for all people. There is no objectively right or wrong way to live; no good or evil. Life has no inherent meaning; it just means whatever you want it to mean. Morality is not some eternal structure handed down to us from above but is just something we made up on the fly. Nihilism is the only truth.

Vlad: Glad to see you're getting with the Christmas spirit.

Idi: Elf!

Vlad: Elf?

Idi: Elf means eleven in German. Idiot.

Vlad: Ah. I should've known you'd want to pontificate in as many languages as possible.

Idi: Mein elf objection! Religious people always seem to be on the wrong side of every diversity battle ever. Supporting slavery; oppressing women; repressing sexuality. Why can't we just let the yuletide be gay?

> *Vlad begins to hum to the tune of "Have Yourself a Merry Little Christmas."*

Idi: Religion constantly seems to over-emphasize the unity of the masses, wiping out any diversity and suppressing every difference. God seems to ignore any oddity that doesn't fit in the offering box.

Vlad: Your very existence in the church undermines that objection, Idi, because you're the weirdest person I know.

> *Idi's eyes search around for his next point, then suddenly blaze with excitement.*

Idi: Twelve! The Father, Son, and Holy Spirit!

Vlad: You already said that one.

Idi: Na uh. I complained that the Trinity didn't make any sense; one plus one plus one does not equal one! That was my former complaint. But this is a totally different issue.

Vlad: Then what is it?

Idi: Father, Son, and Holy Ghost. Do you notice anything?

Vlad: What?

Idi: Where are all the *women*?!? The Trinity is three men! Is there nothing feminine about the divine, nothing female at the heart of the cosmos? That cannot possibly be true. Heaven is not a sausage fest. Hell maybe, but not heaven.

Vlad: Who says the Holy Ghost is male? Why can't ghosts be female?

Idi: Seriously? Have you ever seen a female ghost?

Vlad: I've never seen any kind of g—

Idi: —And now! For my thirteenth and final woe! I ask the one question that all mortal men must at one point or another ask themselves: *what's with all these priests touching little boys?*

Vlad: You know, we're kind of like priests.

Idi: No, we're professors who preach in the university chapel once in a while. Totally different.

Vlad: Tell that to the little boys.

Idi: And I only do chapel when you guilt me into it. I barely even believe in God, depending on the day.

Vlad: So, I'm assuming that if your objections remain unanswered then . . . what? You won't preach in chapel tomorrow?

Idi: Bigger.

Vlad: You'll quit the department?

Idi: Bigger.

Vlad: The denomination?

Idi: Bigger!

Vlad: Christianity?

Idi: Gah . . . Go big or go home!

Vlad: Religion altogether?

Idi leans in real close like he's about to impart some secret wisdom.

Idi: If I don't figure out these questions, my old friend, then I won't go home tonight or tomorrow or ever. I don't want to be one of those atheists who says God is dead and then pisses about with humanism like it still means something. No, I will be an atheist who has the courage to face the void head on! My friend, if I don't get my questions answered, I won't go home to my spouse and my family this Christmas Eve. Instead, I will drown my sorrows and chase my vices and go all out night after night after night, until all my money is gone or I kill myself.

A long silence follows.

Vlad: So . . . do I need to find a guest speaker for tomorrow then?

II

THE THREE

Idi: Merlin's beer! I tell you I'm going to kill myself and all you're worried about is who is going to preach tomorrow. Have you no honor sir!?!

Vlad looks into Idi's eyes and smirks.

Idi: Ya, you might wanna start calling people.

Vlad: Who am I going to find to preach on Christmas last minute?!?

Idi: Well, perhaps you could pray about it. If God provides a last-minute preacher, then great. If he doesn't, then why are you bothering with preachers and churches in the first place?

Vlad: Ya, because that's how prayer works. . . . And why did you jump from having some objections to leaving your family and throwing your life away?

Idi: Because, if my objections can't be answered then there is no God, there is no free will, and morality and meaning are social constructs. Life would be essentially nihilism.

Vlad: But why leave your family? Not all nihilist's kill themselves. Nor do atheists suddenly throw their lives away. People find a way to go on and live well and still enjoy rainbows and puppies and milkshakes.

Idi: And puppy milkshakes.

Vlad: You're a bad person.

Idi: But see, it would all be based on an illusion if I kept on going. Maybe others can do that—and more power to them—but I just can't. I can't go on like it's all ok. I can't go home and I certainly can't preach tomorrow.

Vlad: You know, at this point it's probably easier to just answer your questions than to find someone else to preach.

Idi: Be my guest. Give it a go.

Vlad: Well, there's too many questions. Let's narrow it down and start with the Trinity.

Idi: Sounds good. But I warn you, I shall I put up a fight. I'm like a wounded dog.

Vlad: You know a wounded dog probably puts up less of a fight, right?

Idi: Ruff!

Vlad: Let's get started.

Idi: Onward to the Trinity!

Vlad: To the Trinity!

Idi: To the Trinity, to the walls (to the walls) till the sweat ran down my—

Vlad: —So how can God simultaneously be three and one?

Idi: Yes. All the church councils and all the church men have tried to nuance and wiggle their way out of it, but at the end of the day, there remains at the rotten core of Christianity this ridiculous equation: one plus one plus one equals one. How can God be one but also three? The Trinity makes no sense.

Vlad: I agree.

Idi: You do?

Vlad: Yes. The Trinity makes no sense. At least, I can't make any sense of it.

Idi: So . . . I win?

Vlad: Nope. Not even close. See, I admit that the Trinity seems to make no sense. But what if I can show that even though the Trinity makes no sense, it makes no sense in precisely the same way something else makes no sense. What if I can show a fact—a fact we all believe in—which is equally insane, yet somehow also true? Now, do you remember that conversation we had a while back about aliens?

Idi: That I have a thing for foreign women?

Vlad: That it's totally possible that aliens exist somewhere out there in the universe because—

Idi: —because we exist. Because intelligent life already happened on our planet, so it's totally possible it's happened on another planet as well.

Vlad: Exactly. Life on other planets must be possible because there is life on this planet, and if there wasn't then we wouldn't be here to talk about it. So as crazy as it may seem, the existence of aliens makes as much sense as our own existence. In which case, it's reasonable to be open to the possibility that aliens are real.

Idi: But what does this have to do with the Trinity?

Vlad: Well, what if I could find something just like that regarding the Trinity? What if I could find something that already exists, that's already happened, that is crazy in the exact same way that a three-and-one God is crazy? The Trinity may seem insane, but something like it already exists so it must at least be possible.

Idi: Ok, I get what you're saying, but what are you saying it about? What is the thing that is just like the Trinity?

Vlad: The origins of the universe.

Idi: . . .

Vlad: I want to contend that the problem at the heart of the Trinity is the *same* problem that plagues discussions of how the universe began. The origin of the universe might make zero sense, but somehow or other it must have happened or else we wouldn't be here to talk about it. *Or else we wouldn't exist at all.* And if they really are parallels, then one cannot deny the Trinity for being irrational any more than one can deny their own existence.

Idi: Beelzebub's nose! That's quite the claim. You have some gall.

Vlad: If Caesar didn't have Gaul he never would have taken Rome.

Idi: So, you're saying the Trinity has the same irrational problem in it that the origins of the universe does? And so that explains the Trinity?

Vlad: It doesn't explain the Trinity, just shows that it's possible it exists. If I can show the problems of the Trinity parallel the problems of the origin of the universe, then we can't deny the Trinity for not making sense any more than we can deny our own existence.[1]

Idi: So, if they have a parallel problem, then what is the problem? What is the enigma that both the Trinity and the origin of the universe have in common?

Vlad: Well, we'll get to that. But I don't want to rush, it's a lot to digest. How 'bout we start small and work backwards. Are you willing to indulge me for a bit?

Idi: What else is our friendship built on?

Vlad: To the indulging!

Idi: To the indulging! But first, to the bathroom!

Idi gets up to go to the bathroom. Eight or nine minutes pass before he returns.

Idi: To the indulging!

Vlad: Finally. So what is the problem with the Trinity?

Idi: It doesn't make any sense.

Vlad: Right. And what does it mean to not make sense?

Idi: It's doesn't work.

Vlad: Yes, but more nuanced then that. What do we *mean* when we say the Trinity doesn't make sense?

Idi: That is seems irrational to us.

Vlad: Irrational because it is unproven?

Idi: No, my objection was more that it is incoherent. That's the real problem people have always had with the Trinity. How can God be three and one? It seems like a contradiction. It doesn't make any sense.

Vlad: So we are not talking about evidence? You're not asking where is the proof in the physical world that the Trinity is real? What you're saying is that when you just stop and think about the Trinity, the idea itself doesn't make sense.

Idi: Yes, of course. Proof is a totally different question. What I'm saying is that it's incoherent. It doesn't make logical sense how one plus one plus one equals one.

Vlad: And what do we mean when we say "make sense"?

Idi: That it . . . you know . . . fits within our basic human categories of understanding.

Vlad: Such as?

Idi: Such as logic. The law of non-contradiction, that two contradictory things cannot both be true at the same time and in the same way.

Vlad: And why is that important?

Idi: Because that's how we see things.

Vlad: Ah, now we're getting somewhere. We *see things* through the lens of logic. Logic and the law of non-contradiction are like a pair of glasses through which we see the world. Two contradictory things cannot both be true at the same time and in the same way.

Idi: That's why your teacher won't buy it if you give her contradictory answers. Either you did your homework or you didn't do your homework.

Vlad: Either you paid your taxes or you didn't.

Idi: Either grandma is in heaven or she's . . . not in heaven.

Vlad: Exactly. Two contradictory statements cannot both be true at the same time and in the same way. It's either one or the other, not both. The law of non-contradiction is something so fundamental to our thought processes that we don't even acknowledge it or think about it. We just assume it. Like a pair of glasses we forget we're wearing. So what other lenses do we have?

Idi: Time and space.

Vlad: Right. We are temporal/spatial beings and so all of our experiences are inherently perceived within time and space. I look outside and I see spatial objects flowing through time. Trying to picture something that is beyond time and space would be like a two-dimensional being trying to conceive of a three-dimensional one. Or a being in four dimensions trying to picture something in a fifth or sixth or seventh dimension. Or . . . or . . .

Idi: Or an ant trying to understand a TV?

Vlad: Exactly. Our brains think using the filters of time and space, and so if there is anything beyond that we just can't process it. Time and space are filters through which our little minds process reality, so that's how we see everything in the world. What else? What other filters does our mind have?

Mira: Causality?

> *Vlad and Idi turn to stare at Mira standing behind the bar.*

Idi: *Tim Tebow!* Is Mira interested in philosophy?

Mira: I've done a few classes, yeah.

Idi: Smart *and beautiful.*

Mira: . . . *and* strong enough to shove your face where the sun don't shine.

Idi: I know it's difficult, but with the right stretches—and a little patience—you can in fact get the sun to shine there.

Vlad: So . . . you've been following the argument the whole time then, Mira?

Idi: Ya, you've been spying on us while you are supposed to be serving all your other customers.

Mira: It's not exactly a busy night boys. Most self-respecting people are at home with their families on Christmas Eve.

> *An uncomfortably long silence follows.*

Mira: So . . . causality?

Vlad: Yes, causality. We see something happen and we immediately ask what made it happen; our brains are just hardwired to see cause and effect.

Mira: Right, so like, if twenty bucks is missing from the machine at the end of the night my boss doesn't assume it disappeared into thin air. No, he assumes some jerk-wad *caused* it to disappear.

Vlad: Exactly. Because things have to have causes, and if someone tries to say something occurred without a cause then they are just straight up lying.

Mira: Which is why my boss fired Sandy last week. Because money kept disappearing on her shift, and the only rational thing was to assume she was the one causing it to disappear.

Vlad: Exactly. The only *rational* thing to assume. Because these categories of time, space, logic, causality, etc., are not just true of the external world but are built into the very way we think. They are like pink sunglasses that tint everything we see with a rosy hue. They are how we reason and think through reality. We see everything through them.

Mira: Hmm.

> *Mira says this contemplatively, then slides away along the bar, disappearing into the kitchen.*

Idi: So, ok, I get it, but then how does this all relate to our discussion?

Vlad: You said the Trinity doesn't make sense. I said: what does it mean to make sense? And this is what it means. For something to make sense is for it to fit within our mental lenses. If something does not make sense then it defies our mental categories of logic, time, space, causation, etc. The Trinity does not make sense because it defies one of our basic mental lenses. Specifically, it seems to defy the laws of logic; that things cannot contradict; that something cannot be both one and three at the same time and in the same way.

Idi: So you're saying that the Trinity and the origin of the universe both do not make sense, because they both defy the mental lenses through which humans view reality?

Vlad: Yes.

Idi: But, couldn't you justify anything that way? If you say that because one absurd thing happened therefore any absurd thing can happen, then couldn't that justify believing in anything? Contradictions coming *out the wazoo*, as it were.

Vlad: But that's not what I am going to do. I'm not saying that because one crazy thing is real, all crazy things are real. Rather, I am going to show they are absurd in precisely the same way and for precisely the same underlying reason. They're not just both generally absurd, no, they are the *same exact absurdity*.

Idi: *Bilbo's bottom!* That's a tall order.

Vlad: You've never turned down a tall order.

Idi: Well, get on with it then. Flabbergast me. How are the Trinity and the existence of the universe the exact same absurdity?

Vlad: Alrighty. Now, the origin of the universe and the Trinity are very difficult things, so let's start simple. In fact, so simple, that for a while you may wonder how it all relates back to the Trinity at all. But just bear with me.

Idi: Fine. Bearing.

Vlad: So you see the pub around us? What will be different in here tomorrow?

Idi: Different people.

Vlad: What else?

Idi: Different special on the menu. Different game on TV.

Vlad: Exactly. Even if it's the same pub, much will have changed. You can never step in the same pub twice. . . . And what will the pub be like in, say, a hundred years?

Idi: Gone. Replaced by some better joint.

Vlad: And where will we all be?

Idi: Dead.

Vlad: And Mira?

Idi: Dead.

Vlad: And everyone else in the bar?

Idi: Dead. Merry friggin' Christmas!

Vlad: And how about a thousand years? What will it be like then?

Idi: There might not even be a city here anymore. Hell, there might not be a country here anymore. Perhaps we'll all have moved into space. Of course, that's if we haven't annihilated ourselves by then, which is a big *if.*

Vlad: Exactly. Things begin and end; they are always changing and *becoming* something new. Here on earth, time and change reign with a cruel rod. People are born and die, cities flourish and fade, species evolve and wither, Kardashians rise and fall; time has its way with us.

Idi: "Time's a fire-wheel whose spokes the seasons turn,
And fastened there we, Time's slow martyrs, burn."[2]

> *Idi leans back in his chair, pleased with himself.*

Vlad: Do you just have random poetry you pull out to impress people in pubs?

Idi: I should, shouldn't I? No, it's from my dad's tombstone.

> *A long pause follows.*

Vlad: Wait, your dads not—

Idi: Ya, he's not dead yet. He just always wanted that on his tombstone.

Vlad: Gosh.

Idi: Though maybe he is dead. I don't know. He doesn't exactly come for Christmas.

Vlad: Either way, your poem perfectly sums up what I am getting at here. I'm trying to articulate this realm of time and space and change. All that's here one moment is gone the next; we are, as you say, *time's slow martyrs*. Or as another adage goes: *Man says that time passes and time says that man passes.*

Idi: I get it. Everything changes down here.

Vlad: And since things are always changing, always *becoming* other things, we shall call this the realm of *Becoming*. Becoming is everything within time, all that is finite, fleeting, and impermanent. All that shifts and sands and blows about.

Idi: Pretty standard definition of Becoming.

Vlad: Yes, it is. Now, in my view, Becoming is precisely what we hope to explain when we're talking about the origins of the universe. For it is precisely the existence of this world of Becoming and life and death and time and change that we are demanding an explanation for. I exist. You exist. We exist here in the realm of Becoming. But how? Why is there something rather than nothing? Why is anything Becoming at all? How did we get here?

Idi: We walked from the department.

Vlad: But before that.

Idi: I moved here from Leeds.

Vlad: Before that!

Idi: I immigrated from Russia as a baby.

Vlad: And before that?

Idi: I was a twinkle in my father's eye.

Vlad: And before that?

Idi: My father was a twinkle in his father's eye.

Vlad: And before that?

Idi: It's twinkles all the way down I'm afraid.

Vlad: Right. You could keep going back, until the beginning of the species and living organisms. But what was before that?

Idi: The beginning of the earth.

Vlad: And before that?

Idi: The universe.

Vlad: Before that?

Idi: Whatever caused the big bang.

Vlad: And what caused that cause?

Idi: Another cause.

Vlad: And what caused the cause of the cause?

Idi: The cause's cause's cause's cause. Duh.

Vlad: And what caused the cause's cause's cause's cause?

Idi: It was caused by the cause's cause's cause's cause's cause.

> *This continued on absurdly longer than it should have before finally*
> . . .

Vlad: And so, you keep going back in this infinite chain of Becoming—where one thing was caused by another which was caused by another which was caused by another—and so you never really get to the beginning of all this Becoming.

> *Mira approaches.*

Mira: Ready to order yet?

Idi: I just can't decide what to get.

> *Mira looks down at the menu, unopened and untouched, in front of Idi.*

Mira: You haven't even looked at your menu yet!

Idi: We are too busy unveiling the enigmas of existence to bother with menus! We dare not be distracted from our quest by the fleshly things of mortal men!

Mira: I'll come back. Again.

Vlad: So, it doesn't make sense that the past is infinite. You can't just keep having Becoming explain even more Becoming. You can't just keep going backwards, with the cause causing the cause causing the cause on into infinity.

Idi: But why not? Why can't it just keep going back and back with no beginning.

Vlad: Well, if someone said they would give me a cheeseburger after an infinite period of time had elapsed, would I ever receive it?

Idi: Well . . . no.

Vlad: And why's that?

Idi: Because an infinite amount of time would have to occur first.

Vlad: Exactly. And it's the same thing with the universe. If the universe had always existed, an infinite amount of time would have to have occurred before this moment. History would never have reached this point and, infinitely worse, I would never get my cheeseburger.

Idi: Well you might still get it, it would just take a really long time. So long that by the time you got it, it would be moldy and decomposing. Unless it's from McDonald's, in which case it would look exactly the same.

Vlad: Ah, but see, you're not really thinking of infinity. You're thinking of just a really long period of time. Say, 199 trillion years. But that's not actually infinite. That's just a very large *finite* number. Infinite does not mean "a lot" but rather "non-finite," a number that cannot be reached by finite addition. You could count on and on and on, 1 . . . 2 . . . 3 . . . 19,348,844 . . . 19,348,845 . . . and you'd still never reach it. Infinity is qualitatively distinct from normal finite numbers. No matter how long you live, no cheeseburgers are coming.

Idi: What would a world without cheeseburgers even be like?

Vlad: Godless.

Idi: Mira! I've decided for us. Two cheeseburgers!

> *Mira slides along the bar toward them.*

Mira: Fries or salad?

Idi: Surprise me.

Mira: And to drink?

Idi: Same as last night.

Mira: What did you have last night?

Idi: Surprise me!

> *Mira stares at him in confusion, as do a few customers sitting nearby.*
> *She eventually shrugs and gets back to what she was doing.*

Vlad: In summary, the past cannot have been infinite or else we never would have reached this moment in time. You wouldn't be here now, in the pub, annoying Mira. So an infinite past is ridic—

Idi: —But, isn't the number line infinite? You know, you can keep counting forever, 1, 2, 3, 4, . . . 89,494?

Vlad: In one respect, yes. In another, no.

Idi: Ah. And for a second I thought this was gonna be easy.

Vlad: You think everything and *everyone* is easy.

Idi: Hardly.

Vlad: So, the number line is a *potential* infinite, not an *actual* infinite. An actual infinite is a total infinite, whereas a potential infinite just increases indefinitely. So imagine a vampire who will theoretically live forever. With each birthday they become one year older, and in this sense their age is a *potential infinite*, for it is increasing *indefinitely* (1+1+1 . . . without end). But no matter how many years they add to their total age, they will *always* be a finite number of years old (178, 179, 180, . . .). In this sense, their age extends off into a *potential* infinite, but will never reach an *actual* infinite. There is no finite restriction to how long they can age, yet they never actually reach an infinite age. No combination of finite numbers rubbing together can ever spark an actual infinite. Do you see what I mean?

Idi: Yes, Vampires are real. I'm on board.

Vlad: So it doesn't matter how long you count, you are never going to reach infinity. No amount of finite addition can get to the infinite. So the universe cannot have existed for an actually infinite amount of past time, or else we never would have actually reached this moment in time today.

Idi: But don't mathematicians use infinity in their calculations all the time? So infinity must be legitimate, because . . . math.

Vlad: Ya, mathematicians do use infinites. But there are problems with that even within mathematics. Antinomies such as Cantor's, Burali-Forti's, or Russell's show that if infinity had extra-mental existence then self-reference would—

Idi: This sounds complicated. Can you just put it in the footnotes?

Vlad: Fine.[1]

Idi: Danke Schoen.

---

1. "Antinomies such as Cantor's, Burali-Forti's, or Russell's show that if Cantor's infinite sets really did have extra-mental existence in reality, then there is a problem of self-reference. For example: It seems to make perfect sense to inquire, for any given set, whether it is a member of itself or not. For certain sets one would hardly hesitate to commit himself to saying that they are not members of themselves: the set of planets, e.g., is certainly not a planet itself, hence not a member of itself. For other sets, one would as little hesitate to regard them as being members of themselves; the set of all sets is an obvious example. Therefore, it seems to make perfect sense to ask the same question with regard to the set of all sets that are not members of themselves. The answer to this question, however, is alarming: denoting the set under scrutiny by 'S,' we see quickly that if S is a member of S, it belongs to the set of all sets that are not members of themselves, i.e. it is not a member of itself, but also that if S is not a member of S, it does not belong to the set of all sets that are not members of themselves, hence is a member of itself; taken together, we convince ourselves that S is a member of S if and only if S is not a member of S, a glaring contradiction, derived from most plausible assumptions by a chain of seemingly unquestionable inferences . . . ." Fraenkel et al., *Foundations of Set Theory*, 5–6.

Vlad: Let me try again. Here's a simple, easy, practical example to help put this issue to bed.

Idi: Take me to bed.

Vlad: So, pretend there is this magical hotel that has an infinite number of rooms.[3] And let's say it's a full house on Saturday night; an infinite number of guests have checked in. But then Sunday morning, nine people check out. Would the remaining number of guests be infinite or finite?

Idi: Well it can't be finite, right, because then infinity would just be some random finite number plus nine. Which, as you said, it can't be, because infinity cannot be reached by finite addition. You can't get to infinity by adding 1 + 1 + 1 enough times, or 9+9+9 or even by adding 9,999+9,999+9,999.

Vlad: Exactly.

Idi: But if it's still infinite, then . . . then even if you take away parts of infinity it's still infinite. You could even take away a trillion guests and an infinite number of guests will still be checked in.

Vlad: Spot on. Now, what if every person in an odd numbered room checks out? So the person in room 1, 3, 5, 7, and so on, all check out. So only even numbered rooms are still occupied. Then how many guests would there be?

Idi: Then . . . there would still need to be an infinite amount of guests in even numbered rooms?

Vlad: Exactly. Half of infinity cannot be ten trillion or fifty gazillion, because then it wouldn't be infinity but just a really large finite number times two.

Idi: So if you half infinity you just get . . . more infinity?

Vlad: Exactly. And that's the problem. Take away half of infinity and it's still the same size. All of its parts are infinite, and so no matter how many of its limbs you cut off it is still the same size. Half of it is equal to all of it, so that means *part* of infinity is equal to the *whole*. It's like saying your leg is the same size as your whole body, or that 2 is equal to 4. Which is obviously nonsensical.

Idi: But that's only a problem in the finite realm! It's only a problem when you're talking about finite numbers like 2 and 4 or 100 and 200. But once you go beyond to the infinite suddenly finite rules need not apply; there can be smaller infinites and bigger infinites; wholes can be equal to parts and parts equal to wholes. Of course, infinity doesn't make sense to us, but that's because we are finite beings with finite minds!

Vlad: Thank you.

Idi: You're welcome. For what?

Vlad: For making my point for me. Remember, I'm not arguing that infinity isn't real, merely that it doesn't make sense to our finite minds. Our bigger project is to show that the Trinity makes as much (or little) sense as our own existence, so if you admit that the universe existing for infinity does not make sense to our mental lenses then my point is already made.[4] So thanks.

Idi: Clever girl.

Vlad: So it doesn't matter if mathematics provides evidence that infinity is real. Because it still hasn't done anything to help it make sense to our finite minds. In the same way, Zeno's paradoxes might provide evidence that infinity is real, but it still doesn't make sense, still doesn't compute in our finite minds.

Idi: Dangit. I was just about to bring up Zeno.

Vlad: And I bet next you're going to try and bring up quantum physics. Some say that quantum physics undermines causality and so shows the universe could have popped into existence without a cause. Now, this is debated, but even if the physics clearly showed that this could happen, it still wouldn't do anything to help it make sense to our minds. Because our minds think in causal terms, so to simply negate cause and effect would undermine how our brains are programmed to think about the universe. Indeed, quantum physics so undermines the mental lenses through which we view reality, that physicists often remark: If you think you understand quantum mechanics, that means you don't understand quantum mechanics.

Idi: That was a lot of words.

Vlad: Ya, but you get my bigger point though, right? All I am trying to do is show that the existence of the universe makes as little sense to our minds as the Trinity does. So the fact that infinity or Zeno's paradoxes or quantum physics defy our thought processes is enough to prove the point I'm making here. The origin of the universe does not make sense to finite minds like ours.

Idi: Alright alright. I see what you're saying. But you still haven't shown how the problem of the Trinity is just like the problem of the origins of the universe?

Vlad: I'm getting there. Be patient.

Idi: I'd be a lot more patient with a slaughtered cow in my gullet. Mira! *Wo ist mein cheeseburger*!?

Mira: I just gave the cook the order.

Idi: Mach schnell!

Mira: It's only been five minutes. Grow up.

Idi: Fine, but where's my drink then?

Mira: You want a drink?

Idi: I wanted it five minutes ago.

Mira: Oh, I'll get you a drink alright.

> *Mira grabs a mug, disappears into the kitchen for thirty seconds, then comes back and places it in front of Idi, who looks down at it suspiciously.*

Idi: What is it?

Mira: You said earlier to surprise you . . . Surprise.

Vlad: I'm surprised you actually brought him a surprise.

Mira: So, you gonna try it?

Idi: Maybe later.

Mira: Chicken.

Vlad: Bok bok bok!

Idi: So you've made your point, an infinite regression of Becoming doesn't make sense. Are you finally ready to explain why the enigma of the Trinity is like the enigma at the origin of the universe?

Vlad: Nope. Be patient. We're only on the first of three sections regarding the origin of the universe.

Idi: Desmond's Tutu!! We're only a third of the way through!?!

Vlad: Yes. Because you're still trying to use Becoming to explain Becoming, i.e., saying Becoming has existed for infinity and so explains itself. But that's just one of three options I need to get through this evening. Here, to help you keep track of these options, I'm going to write them out on this napkin. One sec . . . Here we go:

Vlad: So this is the first option, the Becoming option, where Becoming explains itself in an infinite chain of causal Becoming; Becoming causes Becoming causes Becoming. But we still have to get through the other two options.

Idi: Onward Christian soldier!

Vlad: Since we've shown an infinite regression of past Becoming makes no sense, the question becomes: how then did the universe of Becoming begin?

Idi: Mmhm.

> *Idi begins picking something out of his teeth.*

Vlad: And so, if the causes cannot keep going back infinitely—cause after cause after cause—then eventually, at some point, you have to hit rock bottom. A cause that is not caused. Something that is outside of time and so never begins to exist. Something eternal.

Idi: Mmhmm.

> *Idi mumbles this response with part of his fingers still in his mouth.*

Vlad: Something that's not like everything down here in the physical world. Something that is not *Becoming*. Not changing. Not in time.

Idi: Eureka!

> *Idi's hand emerges victoriously with whatever was stuck in his teeth.*

Vlad: Did you hear any of what I just said?

Idi: Duh. It's not that hard. Either the universe of Becoming has always existed or it hasn't. If it has, then it's infinite, which doesn't make sense. If it hasn't, then there's gotta be some first cause thingy that's outside of time and Becoming.

Vlad: Ok, good.

Idi: But wouldn't that first cause also need a cause? I mean, that's why the whole "God did it" thing doesn't work, because if God caused the universe, then the question becomes: what caused God?

Vlad: Ah, but see, that's my point. If we try to use Becoming to explain Becoming—one temporal cause to explain another—we end up with an infinite regression. However, what if we stop using Becoming to explain Becoming, and use something else? What if there is something outside of Becoming that can explain how Becoming began?

Idi: But what else is there?

Vlad: Being.

Idi: Being?

Vlad: Being.

Idi: Being what?

Vlad: Being as in Being! Being itself. Something that isn't Becoming or changing, but is just sheer, unadulterated, eternal, timeless Being. The second option for the origin of the universe, is Being.

Idi: How does that answer the problem?

Vlad: Because! We're trying to explain the origin of time, of movement, of change and Becoming. But everything in time has a cause of its existence. Thus, if we want to avoid an infinite regression of causes, we must look *beyond time*. We must look to something that isn't Becoming but is simply Being. Something that doesn't begin or end but just *is*. Something that isn't in time but is outside of time; something that is eternal.

Idi: But you said everything that exists must have a cause of its existence! That's your whole premise!

Vlad: No, I didn't. I didn't say everything that exists must have a cause. Rather, that everything that *begins* to exist must have a cause.

> *Idi gives a blank, somewhat annoyed, stare.*

Vlad: Everything in time begins and ends, starts and stops, and so needs a cause of its existence. But what about something that is outside of time? Something that transcends the temporal dimension. You couldn't say it began or ended, because such time-based terms wouldn't even apply to it. Everything within time needs a temporal cause. But if something is outside of time why should it need a temporal cause? Indeed, it transcends such things. Thus, at the end of the rainbow, if you chase down the sequence of causes back far enough, you theoretically should find a first cause; a timeless, eternal source of all life and movement. This is what I call Being. That which does not begin or become anything, but simply is.

Idi: Ah! But do you see what you're doing?

Vlad: What am I doing?

Idi: You're complicating things unnecessarily. For if something can exist outside of time without needing a cause of itself, then why not just say that that thing is the universe? Cut out the middleman. Why bring in a cause outside ourselves when *we* could just be eternal? Why not just say the universe itself is eternal Being?[5]

Vlad: Because.

Idi: Cuz what?

Vlad: Because we aren't?

Idi: Great answer.

Vlad: What I mean is that we are temporal beings. Everything we do, say, and experience takes place in time. Time and space are basic lenses through which we view everything. Our universe is clearly in time: the sun rises and falls, trees grow and wither, youth is soon exchanged for literal wrinkles in time; all things tick-tock along with some universal clock. But the eternal isn't like that. No, eternity is frozen, like an unchanging statue.[6]

Idi: A frozen statue? But why?

Vlad: Because, you see, in order to not need any cause of its existence, it must be outside of time. But in order to be outside of time, there can't be any beginning or ending in it; no movement, no change, no Becoming. If there was any of that, then it wouldn't be outside of time and so would have all the same problems that infinite Becoming had. So, I get that it's hard to imagine, but Being must just sort of exist all at once.

Idi: All at once?

Vlad: Yes, because it never *begins* or *stops* doing anything because that would require time, and so whatever it is doing it is just stuck doing eternally.

Idi: Literally frozen *in* time.

Vlad: Or rather, frozen *outside* of time.

Idi: Hmm.

Vlad: But of course, our universe clearly isn't like that. We aren't frozen stuck like statues. No, ours is a land of change, chronology, succession. We're born, we age, we wrinkle, then one day we belch, topple over, and die. *We exist in time.* So to make our universe eternal Being is to negate the most basic category of time through which we view everything.

Idi: But isn't that what lots of physicists think though? That time is an illusion.

Vlad: Some do, yeah. Some say that time is like a line and all points on the line are equally real.

Idi: I think Einstein said that, or something like that.

Vlad: Ya, he even wrote a letter about it to console the family of his dead friend.

Idi: Ahaha what!? Why?

Vlad: He said that the distinction between past, present, and future is only an illusion, and that all moments of our lives exist eternally. And so every moment of their dead son's life is still just as real now as it was before, because no moment of time is more or less real than any other.[7]

Idi: Comforting.

Vlad: Ha, I know right!? Einstein thought time is kind of like the frames in a movie. Movies are actually a bunch of pictures placed one after the other, moving so fast that it gives the illusion of movement.

Idi: Twenty-four frames per second, to be exact.

Vlad: Right, and it's so real and vivid that sometimes it actually feels like it's really happening for the first time. But it's all an illusion. Every image of every second of every scene is already written and recorded, you're just watching it for the first time.

Idi: So the beginning of the movie is no more real than the end of the movie, and though Voldemort dies in the end, he still fully exists at the beginning of the film. That's what time is like, according to Einstein?

Vlad: Yes. It already all exists; it's all been scripted and set and filmed already, we're just watching it for the first time. Time mushes together the frames of our lives to give the illusion of movement and chance. The current moment, the current frame, may *seem* real, but it is no more real than one hour from now or two minutes ago.

Idi: And so you should no more mourn the death of Robin Williams than you mourn the end credits rolling on *Mrs. Doubtfire*?

Vlad: Yes, you've got it.

Idi: But if that's true, then we don't need to explain the existence of our cosmos of time and Becoming, because it's all an illusion. There is no Becoming. All is Being.

Vlad: Yes. If Einstein's right then we may feel like things are happening in the moment, but they've already been written down in the script of eternity. We're just watching the film of our lives for the first time.

Idi: So, what would you say to that? How does Einstein effect your argument?

Vlad: Well, I don't think he does. First of all, physicists and philosophers still debate this, so it's not clear-cut. But more importantly . . .

Vlad pauses to scratch his neck beard, momentarily wishing he had time to wax it so it would stop coming in so quickly.

Vlad: . . . even if Einstein is correct, it still wouldn't get around the issue.

Idi: Oh? How's that?

Vlad: Because even if time is an illusion, it still doesn't explain why we experience the illusion in time.

Idi: Wait, . . . what?

Vlad: Even if I grant that time is an illusion, the question still remains: *what started the illusion?* Because even if we are progressing through a pre-written time, the question remains what kickstarted our minds progressing through it? And so temporal Becoming is still a factor, even if it's just in our own heads. You've just relocated the problem from the universe to our brains.

Idi: So what?

Vlad: So the same problem of the origins of the universe in time reoccurs with the origins of the illusion of time in our minds. Even if you can doubt that time is real, you cannot doubt that you are having your doubts in a temporal way. I *age* therefore I am. And so you haven't answered the problem just relocated it from the physical universe to your mind. *We can doubt time as an illusion, but we cannot doubt that we are having the illusion in time.*

> *Idi gives him another blank look.*

Vlad: In other words, even if the movie has already been made, and the beginning is as real as the end, you still need to explain who popped it into the DVD player to watch it and why they decided to watch it when they did. Why watch the movie tonight? Why not yesterday? Why not tomorrow? Time may be frozen, but you still need to explain why we seem to be progressing through this frozen time, just as all the seconds of a movie may already exist but you still need to explain why we are currently watching Luke Skywalker kiss his sister instead of in another frame watching his hand get cut off. Even if it is an illusion, why are we at this point in the illusion instead of at some other point?

Idi: Clever Girl.

Vlad: Plus, time is one of the mental lenses through which we make sense of the external world; we see and act and think in time. So to say that time is an illusion is pretty much to just negate how we see and think about reality.[8] And since our discussion is not about what evidence shows, but about what makes sense to our minds, this is enough to make my point. For even if time is disproved by modern physics, that still does not help things make any sense to us and our mental lenses. Which is all I need to show for the argument I am making, remember? Thus, while we need a source of eternal Being, that source must be outside of us, for if our universe was itself eternal then that would defy our mental lens of time.

Idi: Clever girl. I get what you're getting at.

Vlad: Finally.

Idi: Though I'm surprised you haven't been objecting to me calling you a "clever girl."

Vlad: What's wrong with being clever?

Mira: Or with being a girl?

> *Mira interjects, as she lays two burgers on the table with a mockingly girlish curtsy.*

Idi: You've done it, Mira! My God I don't know how, but you've done it!!

Mira: What?

Idi: They said it couldn't be done! They said it was impossible, but here is the living proof!

> *Idi takes a giant bite of his cheeseburger then precedes to speak with his mouth full.*

Idi: You've traversed the infinite! I've finally got my cheeseburger!

Vlad: It's ok Mira, he's just being an idiot. It's something we were talking about earlier.

Idi: You two talked about me being an idiot earlier?

> *Idi smiles and takes another aggressive bite of his cheeseburger.*

Vlad: I give up.

> *Idi laughs in response, but his laughter quickly transitions into a cough. He continues coughing in rough fits for a while then starts beating his chest to clear it.*

Vlad: Are you ok?!?

Idi: . . . burger went down the wrong pipe. I need a drink.

> *Idi rasps out these words, desperately reaching for his drink, taking in a mouthful. His eyes immediately bulge and his cheeks puff out in disgust, as he spews the entire content of his mouth back onto the table.*

Idi: CHICKEN BROTH!!

Five minutes later—after Vlad and Mira have both had a chuckle at Idi's expense—the conversation gets back on track.

Vlad: Now that mess is all cleaned up, can we continue with our broader argument?

Idi: Fine. But I intend to be an ogre about it from here on out.

Vlad: As opposed to what you were being before?

Idi grunts.

Mira: I see that his "surprise" has not humbled him in the slightest.

Mira chimes in jovially as she passes on her way to the kitchen, leaving behind two actual drinks on their table. Idi yells after her as he puffs out his chest.

Idi: You've merely poked the bear. I was hibernating, but now I'm coming claws out to show everyone whose king of the forest. Prepare for shock and awe. Yippee kai yay m—

Vlad: —she's not in the room anymore mate . . .

Idi: Grrrr.

Vlad: Continuing the argument. So our universe of Becoming needs an explanation. The causes cannot just infinitely regress back in time, so at some point there had to be a first cause that was outside of time. And this thing that is outside of time we called Being. If Becoming is temporal, Being is eternal. If Becoming is changing, Being is unchanging. If Becoming is within time and space, Being is outside of time and space.

Idi: Right. We need a rock-bottom source of eternal Being or else you end up with an infinite regression of causes. But that source of Being cannot be our universe itself, because then our universe would be outside of time, which would undermine our experience and mental lens of time. And so that source of Being must be external to our universe.

Vlad: Yes, spot on. And that's the second option for how the universe got here: Being. Here, let me write it out on the napkin . . .

Idi: To be clear though, how exactly are you using Being? Because different people use it differently. Being according to Scotus, Heidegger, or Aquinas are very different things. Are you using it to mean substance or existence or . . . what exactly?

Vlad: I guess I am not using Being in the same way they used it. I'm more just using Being to refer to anything that is not Becoming. Anything that is timeless, eternal, atemporal, etc.

Idi: Then why don't you use a different word than Being to avoid confusion with how others have used it?

Vlad: Because.

Idi: Because what?

Vlad: Because I like the alliteration of *Being* and *Becoming*.

Idi: Ha! But surely clarity is more important.

Vlad: More important than beauty?

Mira: Aww. You guys banter like an old married couple.

Mira laughs as she passes by with someone else's order. Idi turns to Vlad and whispers quietly.

Idi: Do you think I have a chance with her?

Vlad: You already know what I think. Go home.

Idi: But she makes me feel young again. Like a wee bopper. A whippersnapper. A fifty-year old baby Yoda.

Vlad: You know Jamie is probably up and worried sick about where you are. I'm surprised you haven't gotten a ton of calls yet.

Idi: Oh I've been getting calls from the old ball & chain. I'm just not picking up.

Vlad: How are we friends?

Idi: So, do you think I have a shot with Mira?

Vlad: No. And besides, it doesn't matter yet. You promised not to do anything stupid until I was done my argument. Let me finish, then you can ruin Christmas.

Idi: You're a real Grinch. You know?

Vlad: Ya, *I'm* the Grinch.

Idi makes a face instead of retorting.

Vlad: Idi . . . why are you so eager to throw your life away?

Idi: If one is going to sin, sin boldly.

Vlad: So our universe of time cannot be eternal but must have been created. And whatever created our universe cannot stretch infinitely back but must be an eternal Being that is outside of time. And this timeless Being cannot be our universe itself, because we are clearly in time, so that would defy our mental lens of time. Thus, a timeless Being beyond our universe must have created our universe of time. *Comprende?*

Idi: Yep.

Vlad: But there's a problem.

Idi: What's the problem?

Vlad: The problem, my friend, is how can something that is outside of time *begin* to cause an effect within time?

> *Vlad takes a swig of his drink then continues eagerly.*

Vlad: How can Being give birth to Becoming? How can that which is timeless suddenly *begin* to create time? You can't talk about something *beginning* to create time, because then time already exists. See, in order to avoid an infinite regression, we had to elevate Being above and beyond time. But then how can it *begin* to create the world? How can something atemporal cause a temporal effect?

Mira: Could you rephrase that? I think I get why a temporal effect can't arise from an atemporal source, but I want to make sure I've got it right.

> *Once more, Idi and Vlad turn and stare at Mira, who has just popped up behind the bar, seemingly out of nowhere.*

Mira: At least I think I get it. Atemporal means not temporal, right? Like, not in time, not within the temporary; the temporal. So it's just a fancy word for timeless?

Idi: *Origen's Knife!* So you really are listening then? You weren't just pulling our chain; you can actually follow all our philosophical terminology and whatnot?

Mira: What, like it's hard?

Vlad: Ha! You better watch out Idi, she could very well replace you in this conversation.

Mira: So, are you going to rephrase for me what you said or not?

Vlad: Right, yes, of course. Basically, how can something outside of time suddenly begin to create the world? Because to begin to do something is to begin to do it within time, but time shouldn't exist yet. We are trying to explain the existence of Becoming, so you cannot just appeal to more

Becoming to explain itself. But unless at least some Becoming already exists, Being cannot *begin* to do anything!

Vlad takes another sip of his drink before continuing.

Vlad: The problem is that Being is eternal, not in the sense of an everlasting amount of time—for this would just be a rehashed version of the infinite regression—but in the sense that it is completely outside of time. See, if it were within time it would need a cause of its existence, but if it's outside of time then it can't *begin* to cause anything at all. So in trying to explain why Being does not need a cause, one renders it impotent to cause anything.

Idi: But what if Being *eternally* created the world? What if Being never began to will Becoming, but *always* willed it? What if creation is not a temporal act but an eternal act, something Being eternally causes. Like a . . . a statue of a baby peeing into a fountain! The statue is frozen, it doesn't change, it doesn't move, and yet it is forever peeing into the fountain. What if Becoming naturally overflows from eternal Being?

Vlad: Ah, but see, if the cause is eternal then the effect would also be eternal. If Being is eternally creating the universe, then our universe is eternally being created, and so everything in it is also eternal, including this very moment in the pub. We would have been eternally stuck having this argument.

Mira: So then it's not just the statue of the baby that would be frozen in time, but the stream of pee as well? The stream would not keep flowing on and on, but would simply hang there midair, as if it had been quickly frozen by a winter breeze.

Idi: Poor little sod.

Vlad: Exactly. And so, if Being eternally creates our universe then our universe would be eternal as well, and so Becoming is an illusion. And if Becoming is an illusion we're back to where we were before, defying one of the mental lenses through which we view reality (i.e., time). And so again, it doesn't make sense.

Mira: Ok. I think I get that.

Idi: But . . . what if . . . what if you don't need time in order to . . . create time? What if there's some other thing that isn't time but is somehow able to make stuff happen? Something in Being that is outside of time but is still able to cause things . . . some sort of eternal factory or motion machine or something . . . .

Vlad: Ok fine, then whatever that is, how did it begin? You can pass the buck or change the terminology all you want; you can call it motion, movement, shifting, swerving, change, cause, whatever you want to call it instead of time, but the same conceptual issue will remain of how it could suddenly arise from Being. A turd by any other name would still be as smelly.

> *Mira laughs*

Vlad: So, once again, temporal Becoming cannot arise from Being. Being and Becoming are opposites; one is outside of time, the other is inside of time. No matter how cleverly you try and mix them they always contradict.[9]

Mira: Is it like trying to mix oil and water in a glass? They cannot mix or co-exist, and so the oil distinguishes itself from the water and rises to the top of the glass. Even if you have 90 percent of one and only 10 percent of the other, they still refuse to share the same space. It doesn't matter how gradually you try to mix them or how carefully you try to rearrange them. They can never co-exist without contradiction. [See Appendix A]

Vlad: Excellent, Mira. Yes, lots of theologians and philosophers have come up with new terms and ways to try and combine Being and Becoming, but it always seems to end up with some sort of contradiction at its heart where something is both inside and outside of time; where the oil of eternity has to overlap—however briefly, however gradually—with the waters of time. That's a very helpful visual, Mira.

Mira: Thanks! I try.

Vlad: So, lets summarize. On the one hand, Becoming cannot just keep going infinitely back, but needs Being. But Being also needs Becoming or else it's just locked up in its eternal cage, unable to create or *begin* to do anything.

Mira: So . . . they need each other?

Vlad: Exactly. You need Being as the eternal womb of existence but Becoming to deliver us in time. Becoming must already exist in Being, in order for Being to *begin* to create the universe. Yet any attempt to merge both Being and Becoming is ultimately a contradiction, because Becoming is temporal and Being is outside of time.

Mira: Right.

Vlad: And this contradiction is what I will call the third option. The "Both" option. The first option was Becoming explaining itself. The second option was Being on its own. And the third option is "Both" of them. Both Being and Becoming teaming up to create the universe; an eternal Being that is also one with Becoming and so can begin to create in time. Something that is 100 percent Being, 100 percent Becoming, and 100 percent Both. Three and one. Here, let me add it to the options . . .

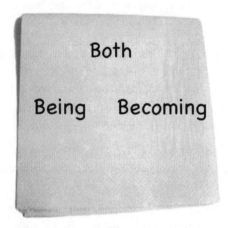

Idi: The "Both" option? Not much of a name.

Vlad: I know. But I told you, I'm all about the alliteration; an old preaching habit. Now, the Both option would be a combination of the two other options. Being would be one with Becoming.

Idi: But, of course, this would be a contradiction?

Vlad: Yes. Or at least, something that *seems to us* to be a contradiction (even if it ultimately isn't, in some way we don't understand yet). In the Both option, Being and Becoming would unite as one. It would be outside of time and yet could create in time. It would have an ultimate foundation of Being from which it derives its existence, yet not be frozen in its eternal Being because it is also Becoming, and so can begin to create the universe. It would be something that is "Both" Being and Becoming. In other words, a contradiction. Or, if not a contradiction, at least an apparent contradiction. A paradox.

Idi: Right, but if the Both option looks like a contradiction, then it's not really an option at all?

Vlad: Oh, it is, just like the other two options. All three options—Being, Becoming, and Both—undermine some mental lens through which we make rational sense of reality. In the Both option, the lens defied just happens to be our logical category of non-contradiction.

Mira: So . . . what is the answer then?

Vlad: There is no answer. Those are the only options. All the possible answers—Being, Becoming, or Both—don't work. All three defy human understanding.

Mira: Surely there must be some other option?

Vlad: Not really.

Idi: Yes really! You can't possibly have exhausted reality in three options.

Vlad: Well, there are hundreds of options, I just think they ultimately all fit into one of these three basic categories. Let me make it simple. I used the term Being to basically mean "atemporal" (outside of time). And I used Becoming to mean "temporal" (inside of time). So you could reword the options this way: the cause of the universe is either Temporal, Atemporal, or Both. Once you reword it that way, you realize just how exhaustive these options are. It's literally either A, non-A, or Both. *Logically*, what other options could there be?[10]

Mira: Ok, I see what you're saying. Let me just double check I've got the whole picture. So the problem with Becoming is . . . ?

Vlad: It leads to an infinite regression, and infinity does not make sense to finite minds.

Mira: And the problem with Being is . . . ?

Vlad: It is outside of time and so undermines our mental lens of time, as well as the existence of a temporal universe of Becoming.

Mira: And the problem with Both is . . . ?

Vlad: That whatever created the universe would have to be Both outside of time and inside of time, at the same . . . time. It would have to be outside of time yet able to begin to cause things in time. Which, to be blunt, would be—

Mira: —a big fat contradiction.

Vlad: Precisely.

Mira: So . . . then . . . ?

Vlad: So then none of the options make sense. Becoming on its own is unfounded; it needs a source of eternal Being. But Being on its own is causally impotent; it needs Becoming in order to begin to create in time. Yet try putting Both of them together and what do you get? Contradiction. At the heart of the universe is this mystery, this enigma of Being and Becoming. *All* of the options are nonsensical, yet one of them *must* have somehow occurred or else we wouldn't exist to talk about it.

Idi: But where does that leave us? How does that get us anywhere?!

Vlad: Remember what this is all about? We are talking about the Trinity. My contention was that the mystery of the Trinity is the same mystery as the origin of the universe. We've explained the problem at the heart of the universe. But now it is time to show how that problem parallels the problem of the Trinity.

Idi: It's business time.

Vlad: So think about it. God is supposed to be this transcendent, all-powerful, eternal, absolute being. God looks down on time and space from the outside, like looking down on a chess board. God is the creator and so is not part of his creation, not down here in time and space along with us. We are tossed and turned by the waves but he is the distant moon that causes them. God is far off in the clouds; God is outside of time; God is eternal; God is Being.

Idi: Right. And he lives in the clouds with a great big bushy beard. Got it.

Vlad: Right, that's the classical picture of God as this distant Father figure in the clouds. But then his Son shows up two thousand years ago claiming to be God. This Jesus of Nazareth exists down here in the temporal world of Becoming as one of us; a real human, spewed from the womb, raised up in a coat of flesh. Somehow, God *incarnates*. He suckles at his mother's breast, cries and whines and poops. He ages, gets pimples, probably has a crush or two. He goes through everything we go through down here on earth in the changing realm of time and space. . . . He even dies . . . .

Idi looks like he is about to speak then stops himself. Vlad continues.

Vlad: . . . And this is the scandal of Christianity. For how can a God of Being enter into Becoming in so radical a way? How can this timeless Father have anything to do with a temporal Christ? How can multiple persons somehow come together as one God without contradicting? Yet that is what the Bible teaches us: that this eternal Father is somehow one with this temporal Christ. God is somehow Both, in some way that no one seems to understand. As Jesus says, "I and the Father are one" (John 10:30).[11]

Mira's eyes get wide, as she begins to recall various Sunday School lessons from her childhood. Vlad sees her eyes widen and picks up his pace with excitement.

Vlad: Thus, underlying the enigma of the Trinity is the same enigma underlying the origin of everything: the mystery of Being and Becoming. The Trinity makes as much sense as our own existence. The relation of Being and Becoming is not a Christian issue we must answer through apologetics, but a human issue that everyone—even the atheist—cannot explain! If this same enigma is common to all, it cannot be a determining factor in considering which worldview is correct (e.g., Christianity, atheism, Islam), for all fail equally in this regard. You cannot deny the Trinity for not making sense any more than you can deny your own existence.[2] In other words . . .

2. Someone might sidestep my argument by simply denying the existence of the universe. Of course, then they'd inadvertently become holocaust deniers.

Vlad takes a sip in triumph before continuing.

Vlad: . . . Cosmology is theology.

III

THE ONE AND THREE

Mira: So, the Trinity is a contradiction then?

Vlad: Well, maybe it is, maybe it isn't. Maybe when we die God will explain it to us and it will all suddenly make sense. But whether or not it ultimately is a contradiction is irrelevant. All that matters is that it cannot currently be dismissed for *seeming* like a contradiction, because none of the other options seem to make sense either.

Idi: But that doesn't prove the Trinity is real! There are three options to choose from! I mean, what if Becoming on its own is ultimately the correct option? Then there is no higher Being at all, it's just us down here in this infinite world of chaos and change. Then atheism is true. So how do you know which of the three options is correct?

Vlad: I don't. But again, that's irrelevant to my point. I am not providing evidence that the Both option—where Being and Becoming are one just as the Son and the Father are one—is true. I'm simply saying that it makes as much (or little) sense as the other options, and so *cannot be dismissed* due to its lack of sense. Since *all* of the options are non-sensical, none of them can be ruled out due to its non-sensical-ness, for they all fail on that criteria.

Idi: . . .

Vlad: Ha. Finally, I've shut you up!

Idi: No, I'm just thinking. I'm trying to digest it all so I can more thoroughly dismiss it.

Vlad: How about an analogy? So, imagine you're sitting on one of those god-awful admission committee meetings at the college. Our university sucks and we need the money, so we basically accept anyone. So, out of the giant stack of applications, almost all of them automatically meet the grades criteria, and so they get in. But there are three applications left that don't quite meet the requirements. However, the school has one open spot left for the upcoming year, and we need to meet our quota. We decide to look at all three of their bad GPA's and let in whoever has the best of the bad bunch. But lo and behold, all three of them have a 2.3 GPA! Suddenly, grades alone can no longer dictate who is chosen. The applicants must then be judged by some other criteria, such as extra-curricular activities, reference letters, attractiveness, sizable donations, etc. GPA can no longer be the determining factor, for all of them are equally weak in that regard. And it's the same thing when we're talking about the origins of the universe. All three options—Being, Becoming, or Both—undermine some mental category of the human mind, yet we must accept that one of them is correct. Thus, you cannot decide which one is right based on its sensical-ness since all three fail on that criteria. You cannot say the Trinity isn't real simply because it doesn't make sense. Capeesh?

Mira: Makes sense to me. Or rather, it makes sense why it doesn't need to make sense.

Idi: Well, the formal argument works, Vlad, but I'm still not certain the Both option really does parallel the Trinity. It felt like a pretty shaky connection to me.

Vlad: Would it help if I went through step by step and show precisely how it parallels the Trinity?

Mira: Yes, it would help.

Vlad: So in the Both option, Being and Becoming are united in one seeming contradiction. Now, of course, we don't understand how that makes sense, but we admit that it cannot be denied due to its non-sensical-ness. And so Being and Becoming are united into Both. Becoming needs Being as its eternal foundation and Being needs Becoming in order to begin to do anything.

Idi: Yes, I understand what it is. I'm just not convinced that accurately parallels the Trinity.

Vlad: I'm getting to that now. So in the Bible, the Father is so transcendent and absolute that you cannot even see his face or you'd die, like with Moses in Exodus. Indeed, the Father fits far more easily into the mold of classical theism; the all-powerful, all-mighty, eternal, absolute, transcendent, Being. So the Father is the source of eternal Being at the heart of all things.

Idi: But the Bible says that it was through the Son that *all things were made.*

Vlad: Ah! Exactly! Exactly my friend! The Son is Becoming. Without temporal Becoming, Being would be stuck in its timeless nature, thus it can only be through Becoming *that all things were made* (John 1:3). The Being of the Father is needed to stop the infinite regress and ground existence, yet it is only in the Becoming of the Son that creation can begin. Through the Son all things were made!

Idi: But if the Son is temporal Becoming then does that mean he is not eternal? Does that mean he is created in time and is just like any other creature?

Vlad: Of course not! That is precisely what my idea solves. Just as *beginning* to create a universe of time assumes that time already exists, so too the Son of Becoming must already exist in order for the world to *begin* to be created. The Son cannot be created but has to already exist in order for anything to be created at all!

Mira: So the Son was never created, but is the means by which things are created?

Vlad: Precisely! Becoming must already exist in Being before anything could be created, and that's precisely what the contradiction of Both allows. Though Becoming is temporal, in its oneness with Being it is also eternal. Previously, no one was willing to make the obvious comparison between the Son and Becoming, because they were afraid this would lead to heresy, for then the second person of the Trinity would be temporal and thus created (and so not really God but rather just another thing created by God).[12] But that was because they were still trying to work within an utterly logical framework. They still thought that to call something temporal meant that it was not eternal. But that is precisely what my broader argument has allowed me to get around. This may not make sense to your mental categories, but it is nonetheless as rational as our own existence. Though the Son is 100 percent temporal, in his paradoxical oneness with Being he is also 100 percent eternal. Therefore, "created" is inadequate to describe him, for *there was never when he was not.*

Mira: Perhaps *eternally begotten* is more fitting?

Vlad: Ha! Someone was paying attention in Sunday School! You really do remember everything. Eternally begotten indeed! As the Nicene creed goes: "eternally begotten of the Father, God from God, Light from Light, true God from true God, begotten, not made, of one Being with the Father. Through him all things were made . . . ." So you really hit the nail on the head, Mira.

Mira: Why thank you.

Vlad: Now, in the contradiction of Both, Becoming is 100 percent its own individual and also 100 percent one with Being, so it can simultaneously be said that at the creation of all things Becoming was *with* Being and Becoming *was* Being (John 1:1). And do you know what tops it all off?

Idi: What? What does? *Get to the topper!*

Vlad: Whereas timeless Being is by definition outside of space and time, Becoming is temporal and so could possibly become *incarnate* and *make its dwelling amongst us* on earth. The Son, as Becoming, can incarnate in the realm of Becoming. When Jesus showed up claiming to be God everyone thought he was insane for God was supposed to be far removed from time and space. But this is precisely what the mystery of the Trinity allows; a God who is Both Being and Becoming, who can be simultaneously up there in heaven and down here *with us.*

Mira: Of course!

Vlad: And though *no one could ever see Being*—for it is inherently beyond finite space and time—since Being and Becoming are one, we can know Being *through Becoming.* The Son can incarnate with us in time, making the timeless Father known to us through himself (John 1:18; 14:6–9) for he and the Father are paradoxically one (John 10:30). When we look at Jesus we can see the Father. Any other avenue to knowledge of Being is impossible for humans, for our temporal nature restricts us to this finite realm. Only through this crazy union of the Father and Son can we truly know the God of Being, truly know what is at the heart of all existence. Thus, *no one comes to Being except through Becoming.* Or as Jesus puts it: "I am the Way, the Truth and the Life. No one comes to the Father except through me" (John 14:6).

Vlad pauses once more for effect.

Mira: Wait a sec.

She whips out her phone, types for a few seconds, then frowns.

Vlad: What is it Mira?

Mira: Just give me a couple seconds.

Idi: One . . . Two . . . What is it Mira?

Mira: Almost got it.

Idi: Got *what*?

Mira: Here! I googled this passage I remembered from the Bible. It's talking about Jesus, isn't it? "Word" means Jesus, right?

Mira begins to read the Bible passage off of her phone.

Mira: "In the beginning was the Word, and the Word was with God, and the Word was God. He was with God in the beginning. Through him all things were made; without him nothing was made that has been made. . . . The Word became flesh and made his dwelling among us. . . . No one has ever seen God, but the one and only Son, who is himself God and is in closest relationship with the Father, has made him known" (John 1:1–3, 18).

Vlad smiles joyfully.

Vlad: Exactly! John 1 was exactly what I was referencing Mira. . . . I'm impressed you remembered that from so long ago.

Mira: Well, that and John 3:16, but everyone knows that one. Oh, and that other one from *Pulp Fiction*.

Vlad: Well, John 1 perfectly summarizes what our discussion of Being and Becoming has been pointing to. As Becoming, the Son was both *with* God and *was* God. Through his Becoming all things were made. As Becoming he was able to become incarnate and make his dwelling among us in time. The Father is beyond all time and space and so unknowable to finite entities, yet because the Being of the Father is one with the Becoming of the Son, we can know the Father through the Son. No one has ever seen God, but the one and only Son, who is himself God and is in closest relationship with the Father, has made him known. And this all makes as much sense as our own existence.

Idi: *Vladimir's Poutine!* This all sounds a heck of a lot like pantheism.

Vlad: No, it's not pantheism.

Idi: Yes, it is.

Vlad: Fine, it is.

Idi: Really?

Vlad: No. *Not really.*

Mira: What's pantheism again? I think I know what it is, but I'm a little hazy on the details.

Vlad: It's saying all (*pan*) is God (*theos*). So pantheism means *God is all.* God is nature, the universe, everything.

Mira: Then yeah, if God is Both Being and Becoming, and the universe is Becoming, then I guess that means God is the universe. But what's the problem with that? Sounds kind of poetic to me.

Idi: The problem with pantheism is that's not how the Trinity is described in the Christian tradition. God is creator, not creature, and so ascribing created realities to God is idolatry. Plus, there are a lot of issues with pantheism. For example, if God is everything, then God *is* the black plague. God *is* the walls and pipes of the gas chamber. God *is* the fist of the oppressor. Pantheism merges God and the evils of this world.

Mira: Oh. Well I guess I can see why that would be a problem. So how would you respond to that, Vlad?

Idi: Yes. Let's see you try and talk your way out of *Pan's* Labyrinth.

Mira: That was weak.

Vlad: Even by your low standards, Idi.

Idi: It seems my wordplay has been critically *panned.*

Mira: . . .

Idi: I'm just saying, it didn't quite *pan* out.

Mira: This is getting worse.

Idi: Yes, things have really gone out of the *pan and into the fire.*

Mira: Let's just ignore him.

Idi: Pantastic.

Vlad: So, in answer to your question: no, I don't think this would be pan-theism. My argument is not that the Son is one with all Becoming, but rather, that he is the initial source of Becoming, from which all other Becoming was made. We are not talking about all Becoming, just the Becoming at the origin of the universe.

Mira: Ah.

Vlad: See, Being is absolute and so cannot be differentiated. However, Be-coming is particular, and so can exist in different and separate forms. The Son exists at the beginning of all things as Becoming, and through his causal and temporal powers of Becoming can begin to create other temporal things that are in themselves Becoming. This does not make Jesus *synonymous* with all Becoming, but simply *the initial source* of all Becoming, like the hand that knocks the dominoes into motion. The hand is not itself one of the dominoes, but it does kickstart the process. Jesus kickstarts creation, but is not identical with creation.

Mira: I think I get it, but can you say it again in a different way?

Vlad: So, the Son is Becoming, but not all Becoming is the Son, just as my wife is beautiful, but not all beautiful people are my wife (though please do not inform her).

Idi: Fine. This isn't pantheism, *per se.* But you are still placing Becoming within God, still making God temporal. The line between creator and creature has been broken.

Vlad: How?

Idi: Because! Time was supposed to be created along with the universe. But by making God temporal—by placing Becoming in the divine—you have broken down the creator/creature distinction, giving God the same attributes as a created thing in time.

Vlad: Well, let me ask you, Idi, what was God doing before the creation of the world?

Idi: "Preparing hell for people who ask too many questions"?

Vlad: Ha! . . . But actually? What was God doing? Because if God was doing anything prior to creating our universe, then some form of time must already exist. Otherwise, God would just be timelessly frozen in place for all eternity.

Mira: Huh?

Vlad: So imagine before there was space. Before there were planets or elements. Before there was matter or the universe or anything. Imagine that the only thing that exists is God. And yet, God can still do things, can't he? God does not have to wait till the world begins in order to begin to act or do things; he isn't that dependent on us. But if God is already doing things, then time already exists before anything else does; time exists before creation.

Mira: Hmm.

Vlad: And even if God didn't "do" anything before creation, even if God was just a disembodied mind alone with his thoughts, there would still be time, because minds think in time. *Mental events are still events.*[13]

Mira: That's interesting.

Vlad: So unless you want to say that God isn't capable of beginning to do or think anything before he created the world, then you have to admit that there is already some form of time in God prior to creation. Otherwise, one makes the very mistake they accuse me of, for by linking time and creation, God almost seems to require creation in order to *begin* to think, act, or do anything. But then God becomes reliant upon creation and impotent without it, breaking down the creator-creature distinction.

Idi: But God could be doing and thinking things eternally! Before time and creation began, God could have been eternally thinking, eternally loving, eternally doing things.

Vlad: Sure, perhaps God does and wills things eternally, but if this is all he can do then he is frozen in his actions—like the frozen statue of the peeing baby—and is reliant on creation in order *to begin* to do or think anything different. Even if God, in his self-sufficiency, may not *want* or *need* to do anything different, it seems unbefitting of divinity that he would be *unable* to do anything different. Further, such a timeless God could not *begin* to create the universe, and so would have to will creation eternally, breaking down the line between creator and creature far more than anything I have proposed, for then creation would be co-eternal with God. So, I think that we actually *rescue* the creator-creature distinction by giving God some form of divine time in himself before the beginning of creaturely spacetime.

Idi: Ok, so then, perhaps time in the sense that we experience it doesn't begin until creation, but that doesn't mean there couldn't be some truer form of time in God himself, which created time is merely a reflection of?

Vlad: Precisely! While created time is just Becoming on its own, divine time is somehow Being and Becoming wedded into one.

Idi: But even so, you still seem to be undermining the classical view of a timeless, eternal, transcendent God.

Vlad: But see, the reason the classical view had to remove all Becoming from God was because they thought this would negate his Being. Logically, Becoming negates Being. But we're talking about something that is not logical; something that is—or at least acts like—a contradiction. In a contradiction, the temporality of Becoming does not negate the eternality, transcendence, or self-sufficiency of God's Being, for both exist fully at once. In the seeming contradiction of the Trinity, God's transcendence and immanence can simultaneously be upheld. God is radically Other in the Being of the Father, and yet can still create the world by the Becoming of the Son, through—

Mira: —*through whom all things were made.*

Vlad: Exactly. So, in sum, we showed that God and the world are distinct. God's Becoming creates the world of Becoming, but it is not one with the world of Becoming.

Mira: So . . . it's not pantheism?

Vlad: Right. But then Idi retorted that even if they are not the same entity, God and the world still share the same quality of Becoming, and so the qualitative difference between creator and creature is lost. We replied that even if God does share some things with the world, this does not negate God's otherness, for this ability to simultaneously uphold both transcendence and immanence is precisely what the trinitarian contradiction allows. God can be both like and unlike the world; able to create the cosmos while remaining qualitatively distinct from it. Far from pantheism, what I am proposing allows God to remain transcendent despite his immanence, a counter-intuitive unity of opposites that only serves to remind us how truly transcendent is the triune mystery. God can be far, like the Father, and near, like the Son, and this all makes as much sense as our own existence.

Idi: Fine. Perhaps it's not pantheism. But where is the Spirit in all of this? You've talked a lot about the Father of Being and the Son of Becoming, but where is the Holy Ghost in the equation?

Vlad: Yes, I'm getting to that. But in order to understand the Spirit, I have to get back to the basics, so stick with me.

Idi: Ok. Sticking.

Vlad: So, we've shown that any rational attempt to mix Being and Becoming doesn't work. Like with the oil and water, they always separate into distinct parts of the glass and do not mix. So the Both option cannot simply be a mixing of separate parts (e.g., 55 percent Being, 45 percent Becoming) but must be a contradiction (100 percent Being *and* 100 percent Becoming). It's not part Being and part Becoming in some sort of rational mixture of parts, but rather, *Both of them at the same time and in the same way.*

Mira: Wait, I'm confused. Why are you talking about parts and percentages?

Vlad: Because, you see, in a contradiction, one thing is 100 percent true and its contradictory is also 100 percent true at the same time and in the same way. But if something isn't a contradiction then they are not both true at the same time and in the same way, but at different times or in different ways. For example, Mira, you work at the pub half the year then travel the other half, correct?

Mira: Yes . . .

Vlad: So then, the statement "Mira works at the pub" and the statement "Mira does not work at the pub" are both true. Just not at the same time and in the same way. Mira works at the pub 50 percent of the time and doesn't work at the pub the other 50 percent of the time. Logical, rational combinations always break down into parts; i.e., Mira works at the pub *part* of the time, but doesn't work at the pub the other *part* of the time. You mix and match and combine the parts, but they never genuinely contradict. But of course, a genuine contradiction is not like that; if Mira worked at the pub 100 percent of the time and also did not work at the pub 100 percent of the time, then that would be a real contradiction.

Mira: Ok, I get that, but why does that matter?

Vlad: Remember how confusing it was in Sunday School when they'd say that the Father was God and the Son was God and the Spirit was God but that they weren't three separate parts of God nor three separate gods? Well this helps clarify how that makes sense. Or at least, as much sense as our own existence. The fact that in the Both option Being and Becoming are not parts helps parallel it to the orthodox doctrine of the Trinity. It's not 50 percent Being and 50 percent Becoming, no, it's *100 percent Being* and *100 percent Becoming.* And in the same way, the persons of the Trinity are not parts; God is not 33 percent Father, 33 percent Son, and 33 percent Spirit. No, there is a genuine unity, such that each member of the Trinity is 100 percent God. Nor can they be split *apart* into thirds and declared to be three separate gods, for God is 100 percent Father, 100 percent Son, and 100 percent Spirit. And that makes as much sense as our own existence.

Mira: Ah. I get it. Well, I don't totally get it, but I'm getting there.

Vlad: Now, pressing on, let us think about what else would be entailed in a seeming contradiction. Imagine you are out for a stroll and come across some strange, new, contradictory creature that is both a bear and a pig at the same time and in the same way. If we were speaking logically this creature would have parts of it that were piggish and parts of it that were bearish—maybe a pig snout and pig tail combined with bear fur—the sort of thing you'd get if a bear and pig made love. But that's not the kind of creature you encountered on your stroll, not by a long shot. No, we are not talking about a rational mixture, but a contradiction. When you look at this creature everything you could say about a pig is 100 percent true. It has pink piggish skin and pink piggish ears and a pink piggish belly.

Idi: 100 percent bacon.

Vlad: And yet, because it is also contradictorily a bear, everything you could say about a bear would also be 100 percent true. It's got big bearish fur and big bearish claws and a big bearish grin.

Mira: We get it. It's a bear.

Vlad: So if you encountered such a creature, it would be 100 percent correct to call it a bear. And it would also be 100 percent correct to call it a pig. And yet, there is also a sense in which it is 100 percent *both*. It's not just a bear and it's not just a pig, no, it's a bearpig!

Mira: Winnie the Poo-Pig.

Idi: The Berenstain Boars.

Mira: Wil-bear.

Idi: Kung Fu Pig.

Mira: Polar Pigs.

Idi: Grizzly Bacon? Gristled Bacon? . . . There's something there.

Vlad: So it would be a pig. And it would be a bear. But it would also be a bearpig; the union of the two, the hybrid born of their merger.

Mira: 100 percent pig, 100 percent bear, 100 percent bearpig.

Vlad: Or in our discussion, 100 percent Being, 100 percent Becoming, and 100 percent Both. Three and one. One and three. Which of course is where we get our parallel to the Trinity; God is 100 percent Father, 100 percent Son, and 100 percent Spirit.[14] Three and one. One and three. God is just like the bearpig.

Idi: Well, that's Kosher.

Vlad: See, while it is 100 percent true to refer to the Father as God or the Son as God, there is also this third entity that precedes from Both of them into one union. This Both-ness is the contradictory *unity* between the two; their oneness, their shared Spirit, the *kiss* between Being and Becoming. Which, as I am sure you already knew, Idi, is exactly how Saint Augustine described the Holy Spirit. Of course, this also makes sense of the churches unity language around the Spirit—such as the *unity of the Spirit*—for the Spirit is relationship, is unity, is intimacy. The Spirit binds opposites into one.[15]

Idi: Other people have said this before though. And the problem with this position is that it always seems to make the Father and Son more real than the Spirit. The Father and Son exist in their own right and the Spirit just becomes this relation that is parasitic upon them for its existence. If two people hug then there are two real entities hugging, but the hug itself isn't a third entity. It's just a description of the relation between them, not anything in itself. And that's what you've done by making the Spirit the Both-ness between the Father and Son. You've made the Spirit nothing in itself!

Vlad: Ah, but that was my whole point with the bearpig! Everything you would say of a pig would be fully true and everything you would say of a bear would be fully true, and yet you'd have to come up with a whole third category of descriptions for this creature. If you saw it in the wild you would not just react to it the way you would react to a pig combined with the way you'd react to a bear. You might oink at a pig and run from a bear, and yet you would not simply run away oinking. No, the contradiction would also elicit a third response of awe and confusion, for how is this creature simultaneously both a bear and a pig? So a contradiction somehow creates a threefold reality. A third reality that exists in its own right, that cannot be reduced to the other two realities. It's not just a bear and it's not just a pig. It's a bearpig.

Idi: I can't take you seriously if you keep saying bea—

Vlad: —So the demotion of the Spirit is precisely what the contradiction helps us avoid. See, if we were stuck speaking logically, then the Spirit really would just be a mixture that is part Father and part Son, in the same way that water is part hydrogen and part oxygen (H_2O). Water can always be broken back down into its parts; a scientist can always separate out the parts of hydrogen from the parts of oxygen. And if the Spirit were like that, then it truly would be nothing in itself but just part Father and part Son (F2S, if you will). But luckily for us, we are not talking about a logical mixture here. No, we are talking about a seeming contradiction. In which case, the Spirit is not composed of parts—not 50 percent Father and 50 percent Son—but creates a third entity that cannot be reduced to the things it's unifying. A bearpig is not part bear and part pig but rather both at the same time, creating a whole new entity that cannot be reduced to its parts.

Mira: So it's sort of like a mother and father coming together to make a child. Sure, the child arises from the two coming together, yet the child is still very much something in its own right.

Vlad: Well, I'd want to be careful to avoid making the Spirit some sort of "kid" or divine "love child" that is born or created in time. Plus, the child language would work more naturally with the Son than with the Spirit. But I get what you're trying to say, which is that something can be the union of two things, and yet still be its own thing. I came from my parents, and yet you couldn't just reduce me into two pieces that perfectly derive from them. I am my own man. *I am irreducible.*[16]

Mira: That's more what I meant.

Vlad: Of course. I understand. So, tying it all together, God truly is 100 percent the Being of the Father, 100 percent the Becoming of the Son, and 100 percent Both through the Spirit, who weds the two into one without being reducible to them. And that makes as much sense as our own existence.

Idi: Fine. But if the Spirit isn't just reducible to the Father and Son then what actually does make it distinct? What gives this Holy pig-bear-ghost its own style and zest?

Vlad: Well, there is so much to say about the Spirit. But I'll focus on just one thing that relates more directly to what we've been talking about. The Greek word in the Bible for Spirit (*pneuma*) is the same word they used for "wind." Now, wind is an interesting metaphor for the Spirit. Wind in the ancient mindset was invisible; you can see the dust and leaves the wind drags around, but you cannot see the wind itself. And if you tried to grab the wind and put it in your pocket like a material object then it would simply slip through your fingers; it was seemingly immaterial, invisible, and transcendent. Yet wind had physical effects in the world of Becoming.[17] Wind could move boats, slaughter man's towers, and rush around the fields, reminding the farmer that he is not alone.

Mira: So it's kind of the best of both worlds then, isn't it?

Vlad: Yes, exactly. To the ancient mindset, there could have been no better metaphor than wind to unite the visible and invisible, eternal and temporal, Being and Becoming. And so the Spirit is sent to dwell within us on earth after Jesus departs, and yet never fully leans to the realm of Becoming—never becomes bodily the way Jesus was—always maintaining the tension between transcendence and immanence. The Spirit cannot be bottled like a liquid nor crucified like Christ, and yet we feel it's comforting presence all around and within us. The Spirit of God is the *pneuma*, paradoxically whirl-winding time and eternity into one swirling gust. O Holy Ghost, who weds Being and Becoming.

Vlad pauses, letting it sink in.

Vlad: Thus, in conclusion, the Father is Being, the Son is Becoming, and the Spirit precedes from Both into one union.

Vlad leans over with his pen, summarizing everything on the napkin.

Vlad: The universe was created *from* the Being of the Father, *through* the Becoming of the Son, *in* the unity of the Spirit. And this all makes as much sense as our own existence.

Vlad finally leans back in his chair, obviously pleased with himself.

IV

3.14159265358
979323846264338
3279502884197
169399375105820
97494459230781
64062862089986

Vlad: You've got food on your face.

Idi: Where?

Vlad: On your left . . . Your other left . . . Ok, now you're just deliberately missing.

Idi: It's not me who has to look at it.

Mira: Can we focus on the question at hand instead of how we handle his questionable appearance?

Vlad: So we've shown the Trinity makes as much sense as our own existence.

Idi: I'm sorry, but I'm simply never going to believe in a contradiction, so if that's what the Trinity is then you can forget it.

Vlad: Well, maybe it is, maybe it isn't. Perhaps it really is a contradiction. Or perhaps it only seems like a contradiction but actually makes sense in some way that is currently beyond us.

Mira: So like you said before, maybe when we die God will explain it to us, and we'll be like: "How did I not think of that!?!"

Vlad: Exactly. One need not commit oneself to an *actual* contradiction to agree with me. You just need to admit there is an *apparent* absurdity at the origin of the universe, and that, whether this absurdity is ultimately real or not, we cannot dismiss the Trinity for currently looking absurd when all the other theories look equally so. But if the term contradiction troubles you, then perhaps you'd prefer *paradox*. My argument works either way.

Idi: Ok. But do you admit you are at least functioning here and now as if it were a contradiction, even if it ultimately isn't?

Vlad: Yes, I am talking about the Trinity in ways that make it at least *seem* like a contradiction. But again, this makes as much sense as any of the other, equally absurd, options.

Idi: Ah, but that is where I really wish to take issue. For I do not believe the alternatives should be listed together as *equally* absurd.

Mira: Why not?

Idi: Because the Both option seemingly defies the law of non-contradiction, which is the most important of all laws. For without this law every truth would also be false. Sure, all three options may be irrational, but the Trinity/Both option is by far the *most* irrational, for it involves a contradiction. And if the Both option is more absurd than, say, the Becoming option, then it is more rational to assume the universe of Becoming has just always existed on its own, and so no creator or God or Trinity is necessary.

Vlad: I see what you're saying. As hesitant as I am to weigh absurdities, I will have to engage with this line of argument. I will have to show that the alternative options are as equally absurd as the Both option.

Idi: Good. Otherwise your whole argument sinks. Not that I'm complaining. I think I may have a shot with Mira, as long as you don't screw it up with any last-minute conviction of my heart and mind.

Mira: . . . I'm right here.

Idi: Exactly. You haven't left, so I still have a shot.

Mira: Like one in ten trillion.

Idi: So you're saying there's a—

Vlad: —Let's compare absurdities, shall we? So the three options to be compared are Becoming, Being, or Both. Becoming on its own would entail an infinite regression or Becoming simply popping into existence uncaused out of nothing, and so that goes against our mental lens of finitude and causality. Making everything into timeless Being entails the negation of time. And, of course, the Both option appears to be a contradiction.

Idi: Yes. And I'm saying that an infinite regression, or something popping uncaused out of nothing, or the rejection of time, while all negating some part of our mental lenses, are still less crazy than a contradiction. That's why mathematicians might embrace the absurdity of infinities, and quantum physicists might accept the breakdown of causality at the atomic level, but neither of them would ever be willing to accept a contradiction. Not all absurdities are created equal.

Vlad: So the terms of the debate are clear. If you are right, and the contradiction of Both really is more absurd than the other options, then the Trinity no longer makes *as much sense* as our own existence and my argument fails.

Idi: Yep.

Vlad: Ok. Then getting started; how is it that you know the law of non-contradiction is true?

Idi: Because . . . it's obvious.

Vlad: But how is it obvious? Is there some sort of argument to prove it?

Idi: Of course I can't prove it. Because any attempt to prove or disprove it already assumes it. If someone says the law is false, then that presupposes that true and false are real things. But if contradictions are real than something could be true and false at the same time. So to try and say the law of non-contradiction is true or false already assumes it is true, because true and false only make sense if the law is already assumed. It's like asking someone if they can hear you on the phone; even if they respond "No" they have, in a sense, responded "Yes."

Vlad: But the man who denies the law of non-contradiction should be quite happy to also affirm it. And if you say that's a contradiction he will smile and say: "So what?" See, it's only the man who maintains the law that can't understand how you can both reject it and affirm it at the same time.

Idi: *Clever girl.*

Vlad: Though I do understand what you're trying to say: you have to assume the law of non-contradiction before you can even get started. But can you also admit what I'm saying? That there is no proof for the law of non-contradiction, for any attempt to prove it is ultimately circular.[18]

Idi: Yes, I'll admit that there is technically no way to prove it. But that's only because non-contradiction is so fundamental. There is nothing higher that we could use to prove its existence, for it is already the highest law. A king does not need to be crowned by a jester.

Vlad: Granted. But could we not say the same for the other options? Could we not say that time, space, and causality might not be provable but that is because they too are fundamental? I mean, how could one prove the existence of the law of causality? For whatever evidence *caused* us to believe or disbelieve in causality would inadvertently assume it, by the very fact that it was able to *cause* us to believe it.

Mira: Hmmm.

Vlad: And we simply have to assume causality in order to have any knowledge of the external world. For otherwise, there would be no reason to assume that the person in front of me caused my mind to perceive that there is a person in front of me, in which case any causal relation between our minds and the world breaks down, and we can know nothing about the world. Perhaps the perception of Idi just popped into my head without being caused by the existence of a real person called Idi. Perhaps this is all a vision.

Mira: So shall I slap Idi just to make sure he's really there?

Vlad: Couldn't hurt.

Idi: Oh, couldn't it?

> *Idi said with a scowl.*

Mira: So, basically, even if we can't, like, *prove* causality, we just have to assume it in order to even begin dealing with the world. Causality is fundamental.

Vlad: Exactly. And this same type of argument could be made for time and space. Any evidence that we could use to support the existence of time and space would itself be evidence derived from the world of time and space, and so all argument for its reality is circular. If someone questions the existence of the world of time and space, all you can do is kick them in the nuts and hope that convinces them. So at least when it comes to proof and fundamentality, the three options seem to be in the same league. The law of causality and the lenses of time and space are just as fundamental and just as provable (or rather, unproveable) as the law of non-contradiction.[3]

3. **P.S.** If you are finding this chapter too tedious or feel like it's answering a question you aren't really asking, then feel free to skip ahead to chapter 5. Also, I recently discovered you can put a note within a note.[4]
4. Black Magic!

Idi: Vlad, I'm sorry, but you're just wrong here. The law of non-contradiction is way more important than causality or temporality.

Vlad: Oh, why is that?

Idi: Because you cannot even *conceive* of a contradiction. A contradiction is unthinkable. Unfathomable. Unimaginable.

Mira: *Inconceivable!*

Idi: Exactly. No one can imagine a square circle or picture 2 plus 2 equaling 5, because they are contradictions and you cannot even conceive of something that contradicts.

Vlad: Oh, but you can conceive of infinity or the universe popping into existence without a cause?

Idi: Yes, you can. You can imagine you're sitting on the end of your bed, minding your own business, when suddenly—uncaused, out of thin air—an elephant pops into existence on the opposite side of the bed, sending you see-sawing up into the ceiling. Of course, something uncaused like this would never happen in the real world, but it is nonetheless conceivable to your mind. You can imagine it, fathom it, *think of it.* But you cannot do the same thing with a contradiction; you cannot even conceive of a square circle.

Mira: Wait, why can't you picture a square circle. I mean, if you give me a sec, I could even draw one for you . . .

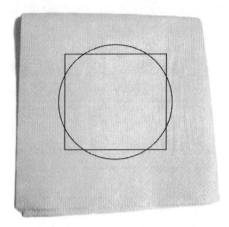

Idi: Ha. For it to be a true contradiction, you can't just put a square on top of a circle, no, you'd have to draw just one shape with lines that are simultaneously round and perfectly straight at the same time. But what you've drawn isn't that. Not even close.

Vlad: Alright. So she hasn't drawn an actual contradiction.

Mira: But how could anyone draw that?

Idi: Exactly. You can't. You can't even *think* of such a thing, let alone draw it. The law of non-contradiction is the most unbreakable law, because we cannot even conceive of its violation. And if we can't picture it, how can it possibly occur in the real world?

Vlad: Ok, so you are saying you cannot even conceive of a contradiction. And that makes it more absurd than the other options because you can conceive of them?

Idi: Correct.

Vlad: But . . . can you? Can you *really* conceive of an infinite regression of past Becoming? I don't think we can. We are finite beings with finite minds, so how could we possibly picture the infinite?

Idi: Easy. You can imagine something going on and on forever.

Vlad: Ah, but if you recall from earlier, that is not really infinite. That's just indefinite. You're not picturing infinity at all, you're just picturing a really big—ever increasing—number. Like 6 Trillion Million Brazilian. But no matter how long you counted, you'd never reach infinity, because it's not just a large quantity. No, it's qualitatively distinct from our finite brain's ability to process things. The brain may be able to picture large numbers, but certainly not infinite ones.

Idi: Fine. But even if you cannot count to infinity, we can still have some vague notion of it. Even if it's hard to imagine, there is still no contradiction in infinity, so at least we know its logically conceivable.

Vlad: But see what you're doing!? You've assumed what you are supposed to be trying to prove! You're saying that there is no logical contradiction in infinity and so therefore it must be thinkable. You've already assumed that non-contradiction is supreme when that is the very thing you are supposed to be trying to show! But what I'm saying is that if other things are equally inconceivable, then you don't have to show a contradiction in infinity in order to show that it's inconceivable. Infinity can be inconceivable in its own way. You can just say it's inconceivable because finite minds cannot grasp the infinite. Here, let me make a picture of it for you on a napkin.

Vlad leans over and begins writing on a napkin.

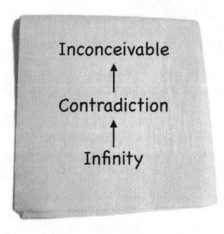

Vlad: On your criteria I have to show that infinity leads to a contradiction in order to show it's inconceivable. But that's the very thing under debate; whether or not contradiction is the only source of inconceivability. But why not cut out the middleman? Why not do this instead:

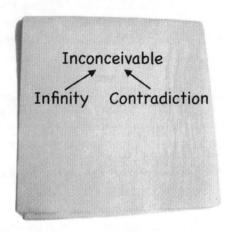

Vlad: We do not need to show that infinity is a contradiction in order to show that it is inconceivable. We can simply say that infinity is inconceivable in the same way that contradictions are inconceivable. You cannot imagine either.[19]

Idi: Alright. I concede your point. At least, I concede it in regards to infinite Becoming. But what about something coming out of nothing or the Being option? Those are still conceivable and so far better than believing in a contradictory Trinity.

Vlad: Ah, but are they? Are they really conceivable?

Idi: Well, obviously I'm going to say yes, then you're going to come out with some argument you thought of in the shower earlier and prove me wrong.

Vlad: Bingo! Now, the Being option on its own means that time is an illusion. But how can you conceive of something outside of time? You can't. Our minds are inherently temporal; we cannot conceive of something outside of time because thought itself occurs within time.

Idi: Wait!

Idi closes his eyes and scrunches up his face really tight.

Vlad: What are you doing?

Idi: Trying to picture something outside of time and space.

Mira: Hahaha.

 Idi exhales in defeat.

Idi: Ok fine . . . I have no idea what that would look like. I give up.[20]

Vlad: Good. Now moving on, is it conceivable that the universe of Becoming could have just popped into existence uncaused out of nothing? To help think through this, let's imagine a unicorn popping into existence in front of you. Are you picturing it?

 Mira and Idi nod in unison.

Idi: Such majestic creatures.

Vlad: So have you actually conceived of an uncaused event?

Idi: Yes. One second there is nothing, the next there is a unicorn.

Vlad: Ah, but see, you're never really picturing *nothing*, are you? You're picturing a field or grass or something in the background. Even if you're just picturing blackness, you're still picturing something, in the same way that the air may seem empty even though it's full of particles. So you never truly conceive of the unicorn coming out of nothing.

Idi: But the point isn't about whether the unicorn comes from nothing but whether it is uncaused. Now, you may have seen the field beforehand, it's not nothing, it's something. And yet, the unicorn itself was still uncaused; some hick didn't drive up and dump it on the grass. No, you can just imagine it popping out of thin air. There is a difference between something coming from nothing and something arising uncaused. You don't need to picture nothingness in order to imagine a unicorn popping uncaused into the field.

Vlad: Ah, but even if I grant that, it wouldn't help you when it comes to the universe. Before the universe popped into existence there would have been *nothing*, and so it literally would have come from nothing. So even if there is a difference between something coming from nothing and something arising uncaused, that difference is mute when it comes to the origin of the universe, because then something would really had to have come from nothing.

Idi: Look, we're getting distracted. Just listen to me. Close your eyes, picture a field, and then picture the field suddenly having a unicorn in it. There is nothing that necessarily connects the second image to the first, nothing that says the unicorn must have been caused. This was the philosopher David Hume's point. In life, one thing seems to usually follow from another; you flip the switch and the light goes on, etc. Over and over again, we have experiences of effects following causes. This happens so often that we just assume things have to go that way, that everything has to have a cause. But just because that is what usually happens, doesn't mean that's what logically *must* happen. Perhaps in some other dimension, causes don't always lead to effects, and some things occur without a cause. There is no contradiction in this. While that isn't how things seem to happen in our world, there seems to be no logical reason why something like that couldn't happen in a different kind of world. There is no necessary, logical connection between a particular cause and a particular effect. There is nothing inherently contradictory or unimaginable about something happening uncaused. Only convention, not logical necessity, links cause and effect.

Vlad: Ah, but once again, you are saying that in order for an uncaused event to be inconceivable there must be some logical, necessary connection between cause and effect, such that to separate them would be a contradiction.

Mira: So it's the napkins all over again! He's still privileging logic and non-contradiction!

Vlad: Exactly. I don't need to show that cause and effect are necessarily, *logically* related, or that imagining an uncaused unicorn would be a contradiction. Rather, I merely need to show it defies our category of causation in order to show it's inconceivable. And indeed, whenever something happens, humans never think it came out of nothing. We immediately inquire as to its source and underlying cause. If the inside of the elevator suddenly smells, we look around for the culprit.

Idi: I don't.

Mira: That's because it's always you.

Vlad: We view reality through the lens of causality. So it's pointless to say that an uncaused event is conceivable simply because it does not violate the laws of logic or because cause and effect are not logically connected. For could we not just reverse that process? Could we not look at a contradiction and say that it is conceivable because it does not break the laws of causality? If an uncaused event is conceivable because it is not a contradiction, why not just say a square circle is conceivable because it does not violate the law of causality? The switcheroo works both ways. The only reason it wouldn't is if you've secretly privileged logic from the very beginning, and so have already loaded the deck. You've already given non-contradiction the premiere position, even though that is supposed to be the very question at hand.

Mira: So, then, you can do the same thing with causality that you did with infinity. Here. Let me add that to the napkins.

Vlad: Exactly, Mira. It is inconceivable that something violates causality, even if that does not involve a logical contradiction.

Idi: Look! Just close your eyes, will you, and picture a unicorn where there wasn't one before. It's totally conceivable. Or picture a deer instead if that seems less ridiculous.

Vlad: But even if it's not caused by the field, is it not, in some sense, caused by you?

Idi: *What*!?

Vlad: You are the one who causes your thoughts. They are not someone else's thoughts, nor do they pop into existence uncaused out of the abyss. No, they are caused by your brain. And so, in some sense, the thought of the unicorn is always caused. *By you.*

Mira: So like how drawing a circle on top of a square wasn't really a contradiction, the unicorn might seem uncaused but really isn't, because it was caused by you thinking it?

Vlad: Exactly. Every thought is caused by the one who thinks it, or else it wouldn't be *your* thoughts. To *cause* yourself to imagine the *uncaused* is like trying to think something that is unthought or perceive the unperceived. You might even say it was a contradiction . . . of sorts.

Idi: That's . . . just . . . ridiculous!

Vlad: What don't you get?

Idi: I get what you're saying, I just think it's stupid.

Vlad: But you cannot have a thought that is uncaused or else it's not *your* thought.

Mira: I think Vlad's right about this.

Vlad: See, Mira agrees with me.

Idi: *Well, what does she know?!?*

> *Vlad glares at Idi. Mira looks down at the table. She swallows, then bites the inside of her cheek, repressing whatever expression was about to spread over it. She gets up, heading toward the bathroom.*

Vlad: You shouldn't have said that.

Idi: I know. I'm an idiot.

> *They sit there in silence for five minutes or so. Eventually Mira returns to the table.*

Idi: Listen, Mira, I—

Vlad: —Mira, what have you done to your hands?

> *Mira looks down at her hands, which are blotted with blue ink. She smiles.*

Mira: Oh, I was just writing something.

Vlad: Where?

Mira: In the bathroom.

> *Idi gulps, suddenly concerned.*

Idi: What . . . did you write?

Mira: I wrote "For a good time call" with your number beneath it.

Idi: Wait, what?

Vlad: Why?

Idi: That's gonna be awesome!

> *Idi laughs, half excited and half perplexed.*

Idi: But why would you—

> *Idi is interrupting by his phone going off. He picks it up, sees it's an unknown number and answers. The excitement slowly fades from his face. He hangs up.*

Idi: She wrote it in the men's bathroom.

> *Vlad and Mira share a laugh together.*

Idi: Alright, have your fun.

Vlad: Wait, does this mean whoever called you is about to walk out any second?

Mira: Oh I think it does. The first of many gentleman callers, I'm sure.

> *They watch and wait, erupting in laughter as a large, balding man exits.*

Vlad: Oh he's cute. You'd look adorable on his arm, Idi.

Mira: I think he can do better. Maybe someone with hair he can stroke while they cuddle.

Idi: I deserved that.

Mira: Yes you did.

Vlad: Are we ready to return to our discussion?

Mira: I am if you are.

Idi: So, I get what you were saying before about cause and effect, but I still think an uncaused event is conceivable.

Vlad: Ok. To be honest, I wasn't totally convinced myself. But no matter. Even if some of the other options really are conceivable, that's fine. Because I can show that a contradiction is also conceivable.

Idi: Ha. Not possible.

Vlad: Oh, yes it is.

Idi: Prove it. What contradiction can you conceive of?

Vlad: This sentence is false.

Idi: What?

Vlad: This sentence is false.

Idi: I heard the words. I just don't know what they're supposed to mean.

Vlad: It's a contradiction.

Mira: What is? What's a contradiction?

Vlad: The sentence I keep repeating: "This sentence is false." If the sentence is true then its false, and if its false its true. It's a genuine contradiction.

Idi: No, its not! That's just a semantic trick.

Vlad: Why? Why is that just semantics?

Idi: Because you can't actually picture that contradiction in your head. The thing about words is they have to correspond to something. So when I say "horse," that word only has meaning because it refers to an actual thing called a horse that I can picture in my mind; an actual horse that bucks and whinnies and carries rich kids through a meadow. But there is nothing real or picturable that corresponds to the words "This sentence is false." It's just gibberish.

Vlad: But you're just privileging *pictorial* conceivability over *linguistic* conceivability. You're saying you must be able to picture something visually, rather than just conceive of it in words. But why?

Idi: Because otherwise your words are just semantics. They correspond to nothing real, like a madman raving about conspiracies that don't exist in the real world.

Vlad: Ah, but at least, in our unique case, one might argue that just the opposite is true. One might argue that linguistic conceivability is actually superior to pictorial conceivability.

Mira: How could you argue something like that?

Vlad: Because we aren't comparing Being, Becoming, and Both based on the evidence for them in the physical world, but on whether they make sense to our mental lenses. Now, pictorial conceivability is based upon the physical, three-dimensional world of visual sense that we encounter. We think in visuals because we live in a visual world. But what do you think Helen Keller dreams about?

Idi: Men with erotic skin textures?

Mira: Nothing . . . she sees nothing in her dreams. She might have dreams but they're not . . . visual. There's no picturing oneself flying or coming to school naked. I mean, maybe her brain could simulate a blob or a flash of light or something but certainly not a proper image. Those blind from birth don't think in pictures.

Vlad: Exactly! Pictorial representation is in some sense based on physical evidence from the external world; we encounter a world of shapes and colors outside of us, then later reassemble these things in our minds to create mental images. But linguistic sense is far more internal than that. You don't need your five senses to think, to have your own personal language of sorts. Helen Keller could think—and write books!—even though she'd never seen or been able to picture any external objects. *Thought is deeper than images.* So there is no clear-cut reason to favor pictorial conceivability over linguistic conceivability. In fact, there may even be some evidence to suggest the exact opposite. Perhaps our ability to speak a contradiction is more significant than our inability to picture one.

Idi: I see what you're saying, but I'm still not totally convinced.

Vlad: Well, I suppose we're at a stalemate then.

Idi: I suppose so.

Vlad: But that's not quite fair. Because even if I clobber you in the argument tonight you could still just say you weren't convinced, and so don't have to go home to your family.

Idi: Hahah. Well, you're not wrong.

Vlad: We need an impartial judge to decide who wins our wager.

Idi: Fine.

Vlad: So . . . how about Mira?

Idi: Her?!? But she hates me!

Vlad: So do all who live to see such times.

Mira: You want *me* to do it?

Vlad: Yes, you. You've been listening the whole time, clearly.

Mira: I may have eavesdropped earlier, yes. I heard the whole thing about whether or not Idi is going home.

Vlad: And you seem interested in the subject, no?

Mira: I had some of Idi's objections myself when my parents used to take me to Sunday School, so it kind of caught my attention.

Vlad: Well then, I think it's clear. Mira shall judge between us, and decide whether you have to go home or not.

Mira: And what do I get out of this deal?

Vlad: How about, if I win—on top of going home to his family—Idi also has to stop flirting with you like a creep whenever he comes in here.

Mira: Ohhh, I like that.

Idi: Fine. But if I win then she has to call me "Captain" from now on.

Mira: I don't think I could judge objectively if those were the stakes.

Idi: Fine. If I win then Vlad has to call me "Captain."

Vlad: Alright, Private. So we have a deal?

>   *All three nod in unison.*

Mira: Alright, well then I rule that Vlad made a convincing case that a contradiction is conceivable, or at least, as conceivable as the other options. So Vlad can move on with his argument.

Idi: Sneaky little Hobbitses!!

Idi: Fine. But even if contradiction is on the same footing when it comes to conceivability, there is still one way in which it remains far more absurd than the others.

Vlad: And what is that?

Idi: It's *practicality*. Practically speaking, if we begin to allow contradictions, the whole world descends into chaos. Once reason abandons ship you cannot save the vessel.

Mira: Why is that?

Idi: Because, if you start allowing contradictions, suddenly nothing makes sense. A guy could confess to killing his mother but also plead innocent, and that's ok, because contradictions are allowed now.

Mira: Children could claim they both did and did not steal from the cookie jar.

Idi: Once you allow a contradiction, all is permissible.

Vlad: But you jumped pretty fast from allowing one contradiction to allowing all contradictions, as if a one-night stand with one woman suddenly meant that all women wanted you.

Idi: I have found that to be true.

Mira: It's empirically false.

Idi: The night's not over yet, Mira.

Vlad: You jumped from one thing contradicting to everything contradicting. But I'm not claiming all seeming contradictions are valid, just this one.

Idi: But once you open the door others will push through as well. Once you say that even one contradiction might be possible then it becomes rational to believe in anything that seems like a contradiction.

Vlad: Just because one contradiction seems true doesn't mean its rational to believe in any old contradiction. In the same way, just because a few guys have gone to the moon, doesn't make it rational to believe that every guy has gone to the moon. . . . For example, . . . Mira?

Mira: Ya?

Vlad: If some drunk guy tried to impress you by saying he'd been to the moon, would you believe him?

Mira: Not a chance.

Vlad: But you obviously know that some guys have been to the moon before?

Mira: Of course.

Vlad: So it's totally possible that out of all the gin-joints in all the towns in all the world, one of those moon-men could happen to stumble into yours?

Mira: It's possible. But there are nearly four billion men in the world, and the odds that I would just happen to be looking at one who walked on the moon is just . . . ridiculous.

Vlad: So just because it is possible—just because some men have walked on the moon before—doesn't mean you believe every half-drunk guy who claims he's an astronaut when he's hitting on you?

Mira: Haha, ya.

Vlad: And in the same way, just because one seeming contradiction might have happened, doesn't mean it's rational to think all things now contradict.

Mira: Hmm. Ya, I see that.

Vlad: Yet let's imagine this guy showed you his NASA ID and you found this whole Wikipedia article about him being an astronaut. Then some random people walk into the pub and start trying to get his autograph. And then, to add to it, his picture flashes on the TV; the local news is reporting he's in town for some event.

   Mira laughs.

Mira: Well yes, I'd be more convinced then.

Vlad: And so, given enough proof from a variety of valid sources, you would eventually be able to construct a rational basis to believe this man really had walked on the moon, despite how seemingly crazy that sounds?

Mira: Ya, I guess I would.

   Vlad turns to face Idi.

Vlad: So we could be convinced that something that seems insane is true if lots of different kinds of evidence came together to support it.

Idi: Such as?

Vlad: Well, there are many criteria that go into considering whether something is true or not; evidence, personal experience, trial and error, pragmatism, intuition, testimony, tradition, and yes, logic. Now sometimes all these criteria work together, and we are left completely satisfied with no remainder. But other times, most of the criteria say one thing, while one or two criterion conflict. In that case, we may be justified in saying that while something may seem contradictory, or unpragmatic, or defy some piece of evidence, it must nonetheless be affirmed, for everything else supports it.[21] There are lots of theories like that.

Mira: Like what?

Vlad: For example, physicists believe in both quantum mechanics and general relativity due to the insane amount of evidence supporting both theories, *even though they currently seem to contradict.*

Idi: But no physicist thinks relativity and quantum physics *actually* contradict! They say they only seem like contradictions because of the limitations in our current knowledge. Underneath it all there is some way they don't actually contradict, and that's why physicists spend their time trying to bridge the fundamental forces; trying to remove any contradiction.

Vlad: But don't you see, that fits perfectly with what I'm doing! I'm totally fine with saying the Trinity is just a paradox and not a real contradiction, and one day God will explain it to us. But an *apparent* contradiction and an *actual* contradiction appear the same from the outside, and so right now, on earth, we have to deal with them as if they are contradictions. And yet, the other areas of our lives don't just explode into irrationality because of it. Otherwise, *we couldn't know anything until we knew everything;* until every little inconsistency was figured out. So we compartmentalize our absurdities. We constantly encounter things in life that don't make sense, and yet we still manage to make rational decisions in other areas; calculating our bills, deciding how much gas we need, etc. We exist in a world with rationality and irrationality, making the best of it. The thinking man has no place to lay his head.

Mira: Or thinking woman?

Vlad: Sure, women can't lay down either.

Idi: No!

Mira: Deal with it.

Idi: Fine. I'll retaliate with this: Vlad, you're saying that believing in one seeming contradiction doesn't make it legitimate to believe in all seeming contradictions, and so some irrationality doesn't undermine all rationality. But aren't you using the contradiction of existence to try and defend the contradiction of the Trinity? Isn't that the very definition of absurdity exploding everywhere? You are pivoting from one crazy thing to another, and once you do that rationality is dead, because you could pivot anywhere and everywhere.

Mira: You know . . . Vlad didn't actually do what he said he was going to do.

Idi: Are you straight-up ignoring what I just said?

Mira: No, I'm responding to what you said. Vlad didn't really do what he originally said he would. He initially used the example of how intelligent life had already arisen once on this planet, so it wasn't crazy to think it could arise again on another alien planet. One crazy thing legitimates another.

Idi: Ya, that's the example he used earlier. Which is exactly where the explosion of absurdity happens, because if you use one contradiction to justify a second one then why not a third, a fourth, a fifth . . . and it could keep going until nothing is rational anymore!

Mira: Yes, but despite what Vlad initially said he was going to do, that's not what he ended up doing. He didn't end up saying the Trinity and the origins of the universe are two absurdities, with one legitimated by the other. No, he said they are the *same* absurdity.

Vlad: Yes Mira! Spot on. I did shift a tad. I used the alien example because it was helpful early on, but I've moved past it like training wheels. My idea is not that the universe exists and the Trinity exists and those are two separate absurdities that just happen to be like one another. Rather, the idea is that the Trinity created the universe, so it's actually just one absurdity.

Idi: Well you've managed to weasel your way out of this one, old sport.

Mira: You really wouldn't make a great Gatsby.

Vlad: So if we start jumping from one absurdity to another then there's no end to it. . . . But! if the triune God created the cosmos, then we are not jumping from one absurdity to another but can honestly say there is just one absurdity. The absurdity that the universe requires is precisely the one that the Trinity provides; a triune God crafted our cosmos. *It is not two absurdities but one absurdity described in two different ways; in the language of philosophy (Being, Becoming, Both) and in the language of theology (Father, Son, Spirit).*

Mira: So you're not saying that one thing is crazy therefore another thing can be crazy too. Because then you could end up justifying pretty much any crazy thing that way, and all rational discussion is over, including this one.

Vlad: Exactly. I've used reason to make my case thus far, so I cannot just throw it out altogether. I have to find a way to reach absurdity without undermining the rational staircase by which I've reached it. The Trinity is not an additional absurdity on top of the origins of the universe but the same absurdity, for the trinitarian God created the cosmos.

Vlad: So we've argued that the one contradiction of the Trinity does not mean the whole world descends into irrational chaos. However, . . .

Idi: However?

Vlad: *However,* . . . I could abandon everything I've just said about containing the contradiction and still make my broader point.

Mira: How?

Vlad: Because even if one contradiction cannot be contained, you could say the same thing about the other options, too. Take causality for example. If you allow the universe to pop into existence uncaused out of nothing, then what's to stop anyone claiming the same thing in other areas? A jewel thief could claim the Queen's crown magically popped onto his lap out of thin air. Just as contradictions could justify practically anything, so too could uncaused events justify practically anything. Thus, the three options remain equally absurd practicality wise.

Idi: Yes, some absurdities may result from allowing uncaused events into the discussion. But not to the same extent as allowing contradictions. For if contradictions are true then all truths are also false.

Vlad: Ah, but the same occurs with causality. You see, if things pop into existence uncaused, then what is to say that our thoughts are causally based on rational premises? We could no longer trust our own thoughts and conclusions![22] Nothing we have said, including your rebuttals, could be trusted. Furthermore, we could no longer believe that our perceptions of the outside world are caused by things actually out there in the world itself. This chair beneath me, Mira serving drinks, Idi sitting opposite me, all of it could be a dream or a mirage that popped into my head uncaused. None of our experiences could be trusted!

Vlad pauses to take a swig of his drink before continuing.

Vlad: And not only is abandoning causality equal—practically speaking—to abandoning non-contradiction, but it may be even worse.

Mira: In what way?

Vlad: In two ways, to be exact. Here's the first: If you punch Idi in the face—

Idi: —Why is this your go-to example?

Mira: So I punch Idi in the face.

Vlad: You punch Idi in the face . . . and that should cause his head to slam back a few inches.

Mira: Oh I could do better than a few inches.

Vlad: So your fist hits him right in the nose, pushing his head back, for the two cannot both exist in the same space at the same time. Fist displaces face.

Idi: So?

Vlad: So that's what would happen if she punched you; her fist would cause your face to fly back. Or at least, that's what would happen in a world where causality reigned. But if cause and effect no longer apply, then what would happen when she punched you?

Idi: . . .

Vlad: If cause and effect didn't apply then when she punched you that would no longer *cause* your face to fly out of the way, and so your face and her fist would suddenly be in the same place at the same time and in the same way. Which sounds a whole lot like a contradiction, or, at least, about as close to a contradiction as you can get in the physical world.[23]

Mira: So then . . . if causality were not real, then practically speaking . . . not only would effects occur without causes but contradictions would occur as well?

Vlad: Exactly. And so it would be *doubly* bad.

Mira: You got all that from punching Idi? What would you figure out if I shot him?

Vlad: So that's the first way that abandoning causality might be worse—practically speaking—than abandoning non-contradiction.

Mira: And the second way?

Vlad: Here's the second: An effect is limited by the contours of its cause. For example, a computer can only create simulations and outcomes that are within the possibilities of its pre-existent programming. In the same way, a logical world can only continue to create logical things, because an effect is limited by the nature of its cause. Like causes like.

Mira: That's why dogs can't give birth to canaries.

Vlad: Brilliant! Spot on. But then if things pop into existence out of nothing, there is no cause or pre-existent nature that dictates what the effect will be like; no laws or logical programming that guided their coming into being, for they literally came out of nothing. Why then couldn't contradictions or infinites pop into existence uncaused out of nothing? If there is no logical womb from which effects derive, then what manner of monsters may come roaring out?

Mira: Alright, so you've shown that the universe popping into existence uncaused is, practically speaking, just as crazy as the contradictory Both option.

Idi: But there are still other options. Perhaps Becoming has existed for an infinite period of time. Or perhaps, the Being option of timelessness. Now, they both might defy our mental categories, but they don't lead— practically speaking—to a world that is quite as absurd as one with uncaused effects or contradictions.

Vlad: Well, as for infinity, if it existed in our daily lives, then all sorts of insane things would result, as I pointed out with the infinite hotel rooms earlier tonight. Some people even think infinity has contradictions latent within it. But even if infinity is not a contradiction on its own, it definitely is when applied to the past, and so is just as absurd as the contradiction of Both. Remember the cheeseburger?

Idi: How could I forget?

Idi says, patting his stomach.

Vlad: If I said I'd give you a cheeseburger after an infinite period of time had passed, would you ever get the cheeseburger?

Mira: No. Because an infinite period of time would had to have occurred first.

Vlad: Right. So even if infinity isn't inherently contradictory, it certainly is when applied to *past* time, because then you would had to have traversed an infinite period of time to get here. But that is impossible, because the finite and infinite are contradictory, which is why finite addition can never reach the infinite.

Mira: So then . . . the infinite Becoming option involves a contradiction, and so would have all the same absurd practical implications as the Both option?[24]

Vlad: Exactly.

Idi: Fine, but there's still the timeless Being option. You haven't talked about the practicality of that yet.

Vlad: I've actually been looking forward to that one.

Idi: You have?

Vlad: Yes. You see, I'd like to contend that the Being option may be the most crazy of all the options, practicality wise.

Idi: Contend away, oh contentious one.

Vlad: Whereas the other options postulate a singular crazy moment at the beginning of the universe, Being posits that our entire lives—past, present, and future—are a lie. Our every waking moment is an on-going illusion.[25]

Mira: So with the Being option it's not just one moment that's absurd but every moment?

Vlad: Exactly. We can keep the seeming absurdities of Becoming and Both isolated to the origins of the universe. They don't have to spread and infect the rest of the world, and so we can still be rational on a daily basis. But you cannot do the same thing with the Being option, you cannot limit it to one absurdity. For it trades every waking moment of our lives to make sense of that one first moment. It's sort of like, like—

Idi: —like selling the brothel to buy a bed?

Mira: Gross.

Vlad: Correct. Gross. But correct.

Idi: I told you. The worse I'm doing in an argument the crasser I get.

Vlad: I'd need a control sample to confirm that. Sadly, you've never gone a night without being crass. Or without losing an argument to me.

Idi: You're a sore winner.

Mira: So, then . . . Being, Becoming, and Both all remain equally absurd?

Vlad: Exactly. And since one of these options *must* have occurred or else we would not exist to talk about it, then it can truly be said that the Trinity makes as much sense as our own existence.[4]

---

4. You might accuse me of conflating the universe with the self when I say the Trinity makes as much sense as *our own existence*. For perhaps solipsism is true, and my mind exists but the rest of the universe does not. Indeed, the Cartesian could argue that nothing can ever make the Trinity as epistemically justified as the existence of my own mind; *I think therefore I am*. In response, I'd say: (1) My argument would still work even if it dealt with the universe and not my own mind, for saying the Trinity makes as much sense as the universe is still a powerful argument in its own right. (2) The Trinity may not be as *epistemically* justified as the existence of my own mind, yet we are not arguing about what is epistemically justified. Rather, we are arguing about what makes sense to our cognitive faculties. Having proof for something is different from making sense of it. The Trinity may not be as proven as your own mind, and yet it still makes as much sense as the origin of a universe in which minds like yours could come to exist. A universe where stars, planets, species, and eventually minds would form. (3) Even if one simply abandoned the external existence of the universe and retreated to personal solipsism, the same issues with how the universe came to exist reoccur when you ask how your individual mind came to exist. Is your mind eternal and thus Being, or is it temporal and thus an infinite regression of Becoming? Like with Vlad's film analogy: *Even if time is an illusion we still have to explain why our minds are having the illusion in time.* Thus, while the existence of my mind may be more epistemically justified than the universe or the Trinity, it nonetheless does not make any more *sense* than those things. In which case, we really can say the Trinity makes as much sense as our *own* existence.

V

THE THIRTEEN

Vlad: Alright Idi, it's time to sneak back into your house in the middle of the night.

Mira: Like Santa Clause.

Idi: What!?!

Vlad: I won the bet. You had an intellectual objection to religion that was preventing you going home to your family for Christmas, getting a good night's sleep, and preaching at chapel in the morning. I answered the objection. Get going!

Idi: Ah, but the Trinity was only my first objection. If you recall, there were a whole handful of them. You've merely scratched the surface, my friend.

Mira: He's right. And you're running out of time, Vlad. The pub closes soon. You've only got an hour or so left for the thirteen other questions.

Vlad: That's less than five minutes per question. It's gonna be close.

Idi: No big deal. It's not like people have been debating these issues for thousands of years or anything.

> *Idi snorts to himself and picks up one of the candy canes from the former nut bowl.*

Vlad: You know, Idi, that candy cane has a history.

Idi: Oh? Has it been in someone else's mouth already?

Vlad: No, I mean candy canes have a history.

Idi: Ah yes. The licorice genocides.

Vlad: Do you see those three stripes that ribbon around it from top to bottom?

> *Idi pulls the candy cane out of his mouth and looks at the three, now smeared, lines.*

Mira: Yes, I can see it.

Vlad: Do you have any idea where they came from?

Idi: Not the foggiest.

Vlad: They were meant to represent the three persons of the trinitarian God.

Idi: Spielberg's Sister!

Mira: I never knew that.

Vlad: It's true. They were a seasonal reminder of the holy presence of the Father, Son, and Spirit.

Idi: We couldn't just let kids have candy. No, we had to turn it into a religious relic and shove it down their throats.

Vlad: The candy cane bears the same Trinity we have been discussing all night; the God of Being, Becoming, and Both, the God whose riddle is at the heart of our cosmos, whose mystery overflows from eternity like plentiful wine, whose paradox hounds us like a loyal pup. Perhaps this is not just the answer to the first question, but to all of your questions.

Mira: I'd like to see you try to pull that off.

Idi: Ha, if you can I'd dare say it would be a Christmas miracle—though I'm afraid I'd only be able to bring myself to say it sarcastically.

Vlad: Well, here we go. Your second objection was the incarnation. How can the almighty, all-powerful, eternal God enter into the realm of time like one of us? Yet in the Trinity question earlier we showed that God can be Both eternal and temporal, Being and Becoming, and that this makes as much sense as our own existence. Thus, by defending the enigma of the Trinity we inadvertently defended the enigma of the incarnation. The cradle is not empty; Christmas is not a crock!

Mira: Right, I guess those two were actually just one question in different forms.

Vlad: Exactly. And did you know why the candy cane has a hook at the end?

Mira: Nope.

Vlad: It was meant to symbolize the shepherding hooks of the shepherds who came to see baby Jesus; came to see God born into the here and now, into flesh, covered in the earthy fluids of a mortal womb.

Idi: Are you allowed to say "earthly fluids" in reference to the virgin Mary?

Vlad doesn't even acknowledge the comment, continuing on with his point, steady and determined.

Vlad: I think that in this way the incarnation is the answer to your third objection as well. You said that religion negates the here and now; negates earth in the name of heaven. And yes, obviously some religious people do that, but I don't think the Bible itself does that. I think the incarnation is actually quite affirming of the here and now.

Mira: How so?

Vlad: Because heaven came down and wrapped itself in dust. Eternity rocked into time. God literally "incarnates"; takes up residence in-*carne*. Do you know what "carne" means? Its literally "meat," as in "carnivore." Jesus took up meat, incarnated in the physical, wrapped himself in *carne*, had a real human body of flesh. What's more, Jesus spent thirty years working as a carpenter—working with his hands, with trees and wood and the stuff of earth—before he ever started preaching about heaven. He dignified the here and now, the daily grind, the sweat on our brows. Even during his three years of ministry he still made earth better here and now; healing the sick, feeding the hungry. And when Jesus resurrected, he did not resurrect as some disembodied soul, but rather, with a resurrected *body*. When we die and resurrect in the afterlife the body is not negated but redeemed and resurrected into eternity. Thus, I ask you . . .

Vlad pauses to take another swig.

Vlad: . . . can there be a story more affirming of the here and now than this? Than the story of God coming down and making his dwelling among us? The here and now is not a hollow nothingness, but a reflection of divine Becoming. Which is why, after creating the world in Genesis, God declares "It is good" (Gen 1:31).

Vlad: Onto the free will objection! Now, watch what happens when I throw this candy cane at Idi's face.

Idi: Wait, wha—

> *Vlad tosses a candy cane directly at Idi, who cringes but doesn't raise his hands in time to catch it. The candy cane smacks him square in the nose, then falls back down on the table.*

Idi: Thanks.

Vlad: You're welcome. There's plenty more.

> *Vlad gestures to the bowl.*

Vlad: Now, did the candy cane choose to fly into Idi's face?

Mira: No. . . .

Vlad: Of course not. I acted upon it. And did it choose what speed it went?

Mira: No. It's weight and shape probably dictated its trajectory through the air, combined with how much *oomph* you threw into it.

Vlad: Exactly. And did the candy cane freely choose to come to a sudden stop upon encountering the aforementioned face?

Mira: Nope. It came to an abrupt stop because of the nature of Idi's face— such as it is—which halted its journey.

Vlad: And did it choose to fall to the floor?

Mira: Nope. Gravity did that.

Vlad: Right. The candy cane only fell to the ground because the nature of our planet's gravity acted upon the nature of the candy's mass. So its entire journey can be accounted for by its inherent nature combined with the nature of the world in which it exists. For the candy cane is an impersonal object. It does not have free will, and so cannot just choose to veer off in another direction midair, but is stuck in its nature combined with the nature of the world acting upon it. Its path is fixed.

Idi: Obviously.

Vlad: But humans are supposed to be different; we are supposed to be personal beings with free will. We think that we—unlike the candy cane— can decide to veer off this way or that way. My path is not fixed; I can choose whether to go left or right, whether to accept a job or turn it down, whether to leave my family or stay with them.

> *Vlad pauses to glare at Idi as he says this last bit, and Idi happily takes this opportunity to butt in.*

Idi: Yes, but it's all an illusion. It may *seem* like we have free will but at the end of the day we're just like the candy cane. We are products of our nature and the nature of the world acting upon us. Whatever choice we make has a cause, and that cause has a cause, and that cause has another cause, and it keeps going back until way before we were born. It's not some guy's fault that he's a loser, because he's only a loser since he has no confidence, and he only has no confidence because he missed that catch in little league, and he only missed that catch because daddy refused to practice with him in the back yard, and daddy only refused because he had back pain that day, which he inherited from his own father's genetics, which itself occurred through millennia of mutations, and on and on it goes. Our path really is predetermined. We cannot rise above and beyond our nature, or the nature of the world acting upon us.

Mira: But just because someone had a bad childhood doesn't mean they aren't responsible for their choices. It might make us more sympathetic to know that, say, an abuser was abused, but it doesn't mean they aren't responsible for their actions.

Idi: Actually, it kind of does. Because every action we've taken is the summation of a million tiny causes, the end product of trillions of atoms, genes, thoughts, moments, and events, which extend way back before we were even born.

Mira: But people go beyond their nature all the time! Good people make bad choices, and bad people make good choices. A poor kid can rise above their background to get to the top, and someone raised with a silver spoon can make a bunch of bad decisions and end up on the street. A guy born with good genetics can waste them away on the couch, while someone born without limbs can go out and change the world. Sure, we are impacted by our nature and the nature of things acting upon us, but we are more than that too. We can go beyond our nature. We are free.

Idi: No. We're not. Because even if we seem to go against our upbringing, whatever caused us to go against it would itself be caused, and that cause would have a cause, and the causes would just stretch further back. There's a reason some kids get out of the ghetto and others don't, and whatever that reason is would itself have a reason, and that reason would also have a reason, and it would just stretch way back before the kid was even born. Thus, we are all limited by our inherent nature and the nature of the world we were born into. Our inheritance is absolute; we cannot truly rise above and beyond it.

Vlad: Right. So the concern is that we might think we have free will, but what if it's all an illusion? In the same way, a thrown candy cane might suddenly seem to veer left midair, giving the illusion that it freely chose to change its course, but when you probe a little deeper you realize it's because the wind was pushing it ever so slightly off its trajectory (or something like that). We might think we made a choice of our own free will, but there are actually millions of factors on a micro and macro scale that led to that choice, even if we can't see them or don't know what they are.

Idi: And that's my objection to free will. The problem of *determinism*. We have no say in anything, because our choices are already *determined* by our inherent nature and the nature of the environment around us. We are stuck on our path, just like the candy cane.

Vlad: Right. Now, let's apply this to God and the origins of the universe.

Idi: Oh lets.

Vlad: So if God is just eternal Being can he begin to create?

Idi: No, because he is outside of time and so cannot begin to do anything.

Vlad: Precisely. His inherent nature of eternity prevents him from doing anything new or different. He is stuck in his timelessness, unable to act beyond it to begin to create in time. Just as the candy cane cannot go beyond its nature and suddenly decide to veer left, so too God cannot act beyond his timeless nature to suddenly begin to create in time. [See Appendix A]

Mira: God is stuck in his nature just like everything else is? So God's eternal Being kind of parallels determinism, because he cannot do anything beyond what his eternal nature *determines*?

Vlad: Exactly Mira! If God is just timeless Being he is not free to create the universe, because he cannot act beyond his timeless nature to begin to create in time. Just as the candy cane cannot violate its nature to suddenly veer in a new direction midair, God cannot suddenly begin to act beyond his nature to create in time. The problem of free will is the same problem as the origins of the universe: how can something go beyond its inherent nature?

Mira: Got it. That makes sense. I think . . .

Vlad: Now, here's where it gets interesting. If God were Both Being and Becoming, then he would have a timeless nature, yes, but would also be able to rise beyond that nature to begin to create in time. God would not be limited by his nature, but have the freedom to go beyond it. Of course, this would be a seeming contradiction, but that is precisely what the Both option allows. Because this God is Becoming he is not stuck in his timeless Being but can begin to freely create in time.[26] And this makes as much sense as our own existence.

Mira: Woah. . . .

Vlad: So God in his Being is timeless, yet he can choose to act beyond his timeless nature through his Becoming.

Mira: Which would be like . . . if the candy cane suddenly veered left midair . . . or . . . if someone rose above the nature of their troubled upbringing and bad genetics in order to live a good life?

Vlad: Exactly, Mira. Exactly.

Mira: And so God is not predetermined by his timeless nature. God has freedom!

Idi: But that doesn't solve anything though! Because the flip side of determinism is indeterminism, which is just as problematic. You might have gotten around one side of the issue, but as soon as you do the other side rears its ugly head.

Vlad: Alright. Why don't you summarize the problem of indeterminism for us, then?

Idi: Determinism says everything has a cause, and that we're limited by the nature of our causes. But indeterminism says maybe some things *don't* have a cause. Perhaps my choices are not forced by my nature but arise uncaused out of nothing. My actions are not determined by any prior cause but just randomly pop out of nowhere in the moment of decision. Indeterminism thus manages to avoid the causal regress of determinism. But it then suffers an equal and opposite problem. For if our actions pop out of nothing, then they can't have a causal source in you as the chooser. So if you punched someone, it wouldn't really be you choosing to punch them, but rather, that action would just pop uncaused out of nowhere. It wouldn't really have anything to do with who you are; it wouldn't be a real, conscious, rational choice that *you* are making. Instead, it would be random, chaotic and all over the place, more like the arbitrary jerkings of an epileptic than an actual choice. So indeterminism is just as inconsistent with free will as determinism.

Mira: Hmm. Interesting.

Idi: So it would be like if God was sitting by himself, and then the universe just randomly popped into existence next to him uncaused. God did nothing to cause it to occur, so could we really say that God freely chose to create it?

Mira: No, I guess not. *Because it would be uncaused.* It would've just randomly popped into existence out of nothing.

Vlad: So, to sum up your objection here Idi, the problem with determinism is our actions are determined by our nature. And the problem with indeterminism is our actions would not be determined by our nature, and so could not really be called *our* choices.

Idi: Booya. Get around that. Since God has to act outside of his timeless nature to create, then it wouldn't really be him and his nature doing the creating.

Vlad: Alright. So to sum up your objection: our choices need to be caused by our nature or else they aren't really *our* choices. Yet we must also rise beyond our nature so our choices are not determined by it. Somehow, its needs to be both at once. We have to act both *within* and *beyond* our nature at the same time and in the same way to make a free choice. Free will, if it were possible, would require us to act within our nature so it still us making the choice, and yet also rise above our nature so we are not predetermined by it. Which is, of course, a contradiction.

Idi: Oh no.

Vlad: Oh yes. Free will might seem like a contradiction but that is precisely what the Both option allows. God's actions are 100 percent grounded in the nature of his timeless Being, and so this avoids the problems of indeterminism. And yet because God is also Becoming he can act beyond his timeless nature to begin to create in time. In the paradox of Being and Becoming, an action can be said to be both unnecessary, and yet still causally grounded in the Being of God. As you say: *Booya.*

Idi: But if it is causally grounded in the Being of God then it is necessary, for anything an eternal Being does it must do eternally!

Vlad: Ah, but in the paradox of Both then God can be eternal, yet also act beyond his eternal nature in order to begin to choose in time, for he is also Becoming. Usually, choices are restricted by our inherent nature and the nature of things around us. Our genes, our biology, our upbringing, our experiences, etc. But in the contradiction of Both, God is able to go beyond his inherent nature of timelessness in order to choose to begin to create in time. Thus, he avoids the problems of determinism. Yet he also avoids the pitfalls of indeterminism, for his actions do not pop randomly out of nothing, but paradoxically derive from his very Being. For Being and Becoming are one, and so even though Becoming is acting 100 percent beyond Being's timeless nature, it is also 100 percent acting within Being's timeless nature.

Mira: Which is, of course, a contradiction.

Vlad: Yes. Or, at best, a paradox. Yet unless something like this happened then we wouldn't be here to talk about it. So free will may not make any sense, but it is nonetheless as rational to believe in as our own existence.[27]

Idi: Alright, I see that. I see how you've justified believing that a trinitarian God has free will. However, that wasn't my main problem. My real issue was whether or not *we* have free will. Are human choices really choices?

Vlad: That was my next step, though you beat me to the punch.

Idi: Punch away.

Vlad: What I was going to say is this: if Christianity is right that humans are made in the image of God, and God is free, then doesn't it make sense that we would also be free? If we partake in God's image like a child partakes in their parent's image, then it would make sense that we have free will just like God does. Humans would just need to have some unchangeable nature in us that reflects God's eternity, and some changeable part of us that reflects his temporal Becoming, and some union between these two parts of us that reflects the Spirit.

Idi: But what would that even look like?

Vlad: Well, if you had to compare the Becoming part of God to one part of the human self, what would you compare it to? What part of us looks most like it is temporal, changing, Becoming?

Mira: Our bodies.

Vlad: Bingo! *Carne* it is!

Idi: Wait, does that mean God has a body?

Vlad: No. It just means that the human body is the closest earthly approximation we have to the heavenly Becoming of God.

Mira: Oh, I see that.

Vlad: Now, if you had to name some part of yourself that most aligned with the unchanging, timeless, immaterial, invisible, spiritual Being of the Father, what would that be?

Mira: The soul?

Vlad: Correct! The soul. Or whatever you want to call this spiritual, deeper self that most of us seem to believe in. The name is not important. The point is, we have bodies. And most people seem to think we also have something else, something that is not reducible to the changing atoms and tissue of the body. A deeper self that remains unchanged despite our bodies getting a haircut, aging, or even losing a limb. Even though all the atoms of my body switch out every seven years, somehow or other I still consider myself the same person. I have a deeper, unchanging identity beyond my changing body. Which is what many have called the *soul*.

Mira: Ok. Tracking with you.

Vlad: So our bodies are temporal and yet somehow they are connected to our soul. But what constitutes this connection? There must be a third aspect of ourselves, which bridges body and soul. Otherwise, our soul could have no impact on our bodily decisions and actions, nor our bodily actions and neurological thoughts have any impact upon the state of our souls. As such, we must have a third "thing" within us, which weds body and soul.

Mira: And what is that?

Vlad: Well, I don't exactly know what to call it. You could call it the connector, the bridge, the mediator, the unity.[28] Perhaps we should call it "both," for it weds both the body and the soul together, in the same way that the Holy Spirit weds both Being and Becoming. So, taken together, there is part of us that is our unchanging, deeper soul, part of us that is our temporal, changing body, and part of us that somehow unites the two together.

Idi: But the soul can change! That's basic Bible 101. The soul can harden, become cruel; or be softened, purified, and redeemed.

Vlad: Ah, yes it can. It can do that precisely because of the contradictory oneness between body and soul. Precisely because the third entity of "both" unites them, the changing nature of the body can impart itself upon the soul, while the spiritual nature of the soul can act upon the body. That's what the contradiction achieves. It means that sleeping with a prostitute really can harden your soul, while a radical transformation of the soul can manifest in better deeds done by the body.[29]

Mira: Ok, but how would this give us free will? I think I know what you are about to say, but just go ahead and say it.

Vlad: Well, imagine if our soul is our unchanging nature. And our body is our changing nature. And then this third thing within us weds both our body and soul into one unified, paradoxical entity. If this were so—*or at least something like it were so*—then it could simultaneously be said that our choices are founded in the inherent nature of our unchanging soul, and yet we are also acting beyond our inherent nature, for we also have a changing, physical body (in the same way that Being can act outside of its nature through its Becoming). Our choices must not be limited by the unchanging nature of our soul, or else we are unfree. And yet, unless our choices are grounded in some sort of essential self/soul, then they cannot truly be called our choices.[30] In the paradox of body, soul and both, we can simultaneously act within and outside of our inherent nature.[31] In the same way that God could freely choose to create the cosmos, we can freely choose to make decisions. We hominids are microcosms of the Big Bang, gushing forth raw choices. We have a cosmological, creative, triune freedom.

Idi: But now you're doing what you said you wouldn't do!

Vlad: And that is?

Idi: You said before that one contradiction at the origin of the universe would not explode and justify seeing contradictions wherever you want. But that's precisely what you're doing here. You are taking the one contradiction and spreading it to justify believing anything. Human free will has nothing to do with the origins of the universe. So now you are letting absurdity explode into different discussions, undermining all rationality and making true conversation impossible. One contradiction has justified others, and the slide down the slippery slope to irrationality has begun.

Vlad: Ah, but see, according to a Christian worldview, these aren't *different* absurdities at all. Christians belief that humanity was made in the *image* of the triune God. In Genesis, it says "God made them in the divine image; male and female God made them." We are a reflection of God, in the same way a child is a reflection of their parents. Thus, when you talk about the creator of the universe, you are always talking, in some small (indirect) sense, about yourself. I am not letting one contradiction explode and justify other absurdities, for as you say, that would undermine all reason. I am not using one absurdity to justify another separate one. Rather, I am simply explicating the implications of the single absurdity, for the absurd image of the triune God also dwells in us.

Mira: So, triune freedom and human freedom are not two separate crazy things, but the *same* crazy thing manifesting in different contexts? And that one crazy thing is, is . . .

Vlad: Go on . . .

Mira: The one, single, crazy absurdity in all the universe is . . . the personal.

> *Vlad smiles.*

Mira: The personal is the one contradiction at the heart of everything![5] Rocks don't have free will because they are not personal, not made in the image of a personal God like we are.

Vlad: The personal is at the beginning of all things and is carried on in us, like the stardust at the early stages of the universe that now dwells within us all.

Mira: So . . . then . . . there are not a bunch of different contradictions but just the one contradiction of personhood? There is no explosion of

5. This may also help clarify other questions. For example, if God's nature is 100 percent preserved and yet his freedom is also 100 percent contradictorily intact, this could help resolve the tension between nature and will that dates back at least as far as Scotus and Ockham, and which has been the focus of so much recent scholarship. Here's another example, regarding Calvinism and Arminianism: If God can know and predetermine our nature, and our nature is contradictorily one with that which freely rises above and beyond it, then God can simultaneously be said to 100 percent know and determine all things beforehand, and yet his creatures are still 100 percent free and undetermined. And as odd as that sounds, it makes about as much sense as our own existence. Perhaps theologians should stop trying to resolve these tensions and instead make themselves at home in them, just as we have all made ourselves at home in this inexplicable cosmos.

craziness, no expanding of absurdities beyond the single absurdity of the personal?

Vlad: Exactly. If creation was a free act, and we were made in the image of the creator, then human free will is not an additional absurdity but the same one that is at the origins of all things. I haven't used one absurdity to justify others, rather, I am still just talking about the same single absurdity.

Mira: So you've reached an irrational conclusion but haven't undermined the rational premises by which you've got there by letting contradictions explode out wherever we feel like?

Vlad: Yes, you could say that.

Idi: *Clever girl.*

Mira: Why do you keep calling Vlad a "clever girl"?

Idi: It's a line from a movie.

Vlad: Moving on, I think I can almost make a new argument for the existence of God that appeals to those who believe in free will.

Mira: How?

Vlad: Well, since free will is rather absurd, taken on its own merits, we really shouldn't be justified in believing in it at all. But if you link human free will with the origin of the universe as I've done here, then free will becomes as rational to believe in as our own existence.

Idi: You've already said all that.

Vlad: Yes, but then think about it. If one has to link free will with the origins of the universe in order to justify believing in it, then doesn't that imply that the creation of the universe was a free choice? Saying our free choices are the same as the act of creating the universe means that the universe was created by a free choice. And if chosen, then there is a chooser. Indeed, none of the impersonal, material things of this universe could ever explain our existence, for they would be stuck in their inherent nature, unable to begin to create the cosmos. Only the free choice of a personal entity could allow Being to act beyond its timeless nature to begin to create. If human choice and the creation of the universe are the same absurdity, then does it not seem clear that whatever created the cosmos must be as free and personal as we are?

Mira: Hmm. I guess once you say that human free will and the creation of the universe are the same absurdity of personhood, then it's rather unavoidable that something personal created the universe, and so . . . God exists.

Idi: Yes, but that argument only works on people who already believe in free will.

Mira: But isn't that most people though? Don't most of us have some strong sense that we aren't just robots following our programming? That our decisions really are our own? That our love is not forced but freely given, and that when we hurt those we love we really are guilty? . . . I guess, deep down, I've always wanted to believe in free will. But I've kind of struggled to find a plausible justification to believe in it in our modern world. Vlad's argument provides some way forward again, a way to believe in freedom again.

Idi: You may take our lives . . . but you'll never take . . . OUR FREEDOMMM!!!!

Vlad: Your Scottish accent isn't half bad.

Idi: Thanks laddie.

Vlad: So, in sum, to justify believing in the absurdity of personal free will, one merges it with the absurdity of our own existence, and so something personal must have created the universe. Though, of course, whether or not someone finds this convincing will depend on what they already feel about free will.

Mira: So it really is meant to be a new argument for the existence of God then?

Vlad: Yes, but not just the existence of God. The existence of a specifically trinitarian God.

Idi: Moby's dick! You really are going for it.

Vlad: I am. See, we've agreed that human freedom points to a free act at the origins of everything. But in order for there to be a free act at the beginning of the universe the Both option—where Being can act beyond its timeless nature through its union with Becoming—must be true. And the Both option is essentially trinitarian (or at least quite close to it) requiring there to be 100 percent Being, 100 percent Becoming, and 100 percent Both. Thus, in merging human freedom with cosmology, we've not just made an argument from freedom for the existence of God but for the existence of the Trinity as well. We've argued for what Christians have claimed all along: a triune God *freely* chose to create the cosmos.

Idi: So, if I kick someone, and God doesn't exist, then it's not my fault because I don't have free will?

Vlad: Precisely.

> *A shuffling occurs under the table.*

Vlad: Ouch! What the?!

Idi: You said it wasn't my fault, remember?

Vlad: *That's only if God doesn't exist!*

Idi: And if he does exist, he'll forgive me.

Mira: You're an idiot.

Idi: And also not an idiot, at the same time and in the same way. It's a contradiction. Yay, look at me, I've solved everything. Wippety doo dah.

Mira: You know, you can't spell "Idiot" without "Idi."

Idi: Yah, well you can't . . . spell . . . um . . .

Mira: . . . You *can't spell* what? You can't spell Miraculous without 'Mira'? You can't spell Admiration without "Mira"? Or did you mean you literally *can't spell?*

Vlad: Focus people! We're only on point four.

Mira: There's no way we're gonna get to all of them before the pub closes.

Idi: I'm gonna win!

Vlad: Don't count your chickens just yet. Onward to objection five!

Idi: And what was that?

Vlad: The soul-body problem (or the mind-body problem). Are we just bodies of atoms and cells? Or do we have a soul? And if so, how does this soul relate to the brain and body.

Idi: And how do you propose to answer that, you glorified meat sack?

Vlad: Well, we don't want to define the soul in bodily terms, or else it just becomes some sort of control center in the brain with physical nobs and buttons to give the body commands. Then it would not really be a soul but just another material part of the brain that science could eventually map. So, in order to avoid making the soul material, you have to define it as a fundamentally different substance from the body. Yet if they are fundamentally different substances, then how can they interact at all?

Mira: But, I mean, my hand is different than Idi's face, yet I can still slap him if I need to.

Vlad: True. But see, your hand and Idi's face may be different things, but they are not composed of different substances. No, they are both made out of material atoms. So, at the end of the day they can interact because they exist on the same plane and are made out of the same stuff. But the soul isn't supposed to be made out of atoms. The soul is not a material substance but rather an *immaterial* substance. So how does something that is non-material—that is a fundamentally different substance—interact with material things? How can a soul interact with a body? How can the soul give commands to the body, or in turn, how can what we do in the body impact the state and sanctity of our souls?

Idi: It's sort of like with ghosts. Ghosts can walk through walls because they are not material beings, and yet in the movies these same ghosts can also slam doors, do pottery, or kiss a girl, and so there is this fundamental inconsistency. Either they are immaterial and can go through walls, or they are material and can impact the physical world. They can't do both. Get it together Hollywood.

Vlad: Right. If the soul can actually impact the body, then there must be some connection between them, such that they are actually made out of the same underlying substance, in the same way that your hand and Idi's face can interact because they are both material substances made of material atoms. In which case, then the soul becomes part of the body, and we should be able to find it in the brain. Then we don't really have some immaterial, spiritual, soul, but just another faculty of the material brain, and so humans really are just a body and nothing else. Materialism wins the day.

Idi: Nature is a butcher and we are sacks of meat.

Mira: So that's the body-soul dilemma?

Vlad: Yes.

Mira: And how do you propose to answer that?

Vlad: The same way I've answered everything else. If humans are indeed made in the image of a triune God, then the contradiction of the origins of the universe resides in us as well. Just as God is 100 percent Being, 100 percent Becoming, and 100 percent Both, we are 100 percent soul, 100 percent body, and 100 percent both. In which case, the substances of body and soul can be both truly distinct and truly united at the same time. This is, of course, a contradiction, but it makes as much sense as our own existence. Previously, in order for body and soul to interact they would have to be consistent with one another; united in substance; woven from the same cloth. But in a contradiction they don't have to be consistent. Indeed, they can be *truly inconsistent*, and yet somehow also united. In this sense, the soul can impact the body, and the actions of the body impact the state of our soil, without giving in to substance materialism. We can be both 100 percent bodily and yet also 100 percent spiritual. We truly are bodies. And yet, so much more.

Mira: So Casper can both go through the wall *and* kiss the girl?

Vlad: Or go through the girl and kiss the wall. Whatever he's into.

Idi: Probably some spooky shi—

Vlad: —Language! You ghoul. Evangelicals are reading this.

Idi: This is getting ridiculous.

Vlad: Oh? How so?

Idi: You're trying to tie up in a nice little bow all these debates that have been going on for thousands of years. You are covering over a whole sea of subtlety, nuance, and discussion.

Vlad: Look, of course this doesn't answer things once and for all. But it does help us realize that the same problems that appear at the origins of the universe also reappear in human free will, the body-soul dilemma, and a whole host of other issues. So even if we can't give a definitive answer, we at least know that our inability to answer no more negates the soul or free will than it negates our own existence.[6]

Idi: Whatever. What was my next objection? I think it was . . . um . . .

Vlad: It was . . . ah—

Mira: Evil.

> Both Idi and Vlad turn and look at Mira.

Mira: Idi said if free will is bogus then you can't fault humanity for screwing up the world, because we didn't have a choice. So it's God's fault that Idi is like this.

Idi: I like how you say my name.

Mira: Do you ever give up?

---

6. There are indeed two ways to take my overall argument. You can agree with the positive case I've made for how the Trinity actually works and all the subsequent proposals I've made about how free will and the body and soul function, etc. Or you could accept only the negative case that the fact that these issues arise in Christianity does not disprove it any more than it disproves our own existence. One need not accept all the details of the former positive case to see the validity in the latter case.

Idi: Mother told me quitting is for losers.

Vlad: Idi's childhood perfectly sets us up for the next question: the problem of evil. Now, one of the traditional answers to the problem of evil is that humans have free will. God could have forced everybody to be nice to each other and never hurt anyone, but then we would all be robots, following our programming. Then we wouldn't even be human, just chess pieces God moves around on the board of life. For love to be real, doesn't it need to be freely chosen? If I lock you up in my basement and force you to love me, is that really love? No, because its forced, not chosen. A forced love is no love at all; a forced love is rape. Thus, God could have forced humans to love each other and be nice and never hurt anyone, but that wouldn't really be love, we wouldn't really be human, the world wouldn't really be perfect. So God has to give us freedom of choice. But wherever there is a choice there must be more than one option to choose between. Wherever there is the choice to love, there must also be the choice to hate. Where there is *significant* moral freedom, there is always the possibility of evil. Thus, free will explains evil.

Idi: Except the problem is that free will doesn't make any sense.

Mira: Right. Or at least, that was the problem.

Vlad: T'was indeed. But now that we've shown that it may be rational to believe in free will even if you can't make sense of it, we can once again use it to answer the problem of evil. So my previous defense of free will also inadvertently was a defense of the problem of evil. Even if God made us and our world perfect, free will allows us to act beyond our perfect nature in order to choose evil. Even the purest garden has its snakes.

Mira: So that's why humanity can have so much good in us—so much potential for beauty, brilliance, and compassion—yet so often choose to pervert our nature?

Idi: So *very very often.* As Satan says in Milton, *"Out of good still to find means of evil."*

> *The table pauses in near unison, reflecting on these words for a few seconds before Vlad breaks the silence.*

Vlad: And yet, God *"out of our evil seeks to bring forth good . . . ."*

Another pause. Idi looks away.

Mira: So free will answers question six, then?

Idi: Not quite. There are other types of evils, like natural evil. What about disease, hurricanes, tsunamis? Those aren't caused by human freedom.

Mira: I mean, sometimes they are. Global warming is probably our fault. And disease often spreads because of government negligence or the indifference of the public. So human free will explains some of natural evil.

Idi: Yes, but not *all* of it. How does free will explain an earthquake leveling a city, or a meteor wiping out entire species?

Vlad: That's a good question, Idi. But not one that I have to answer here tonight. If you recall, at the beginning of the evening you only brought up examples of human evil, not natural evil. I didn't agree to answer every conceivable question ever. I only agreed to answer the specific objections you already brought up.

Idi: *Clever girl.* So you're just not going to answer it then?

Vlad: No, I'm not. Partially because of what I just said, and partially because it's really hard and I don't wanna.

Vlad: Shall we move on to the next point. What was your next issue again?

Idi: Other religions. Why do you think the Christian conception of God is the right one when all these other religions have their own pictures of God as well?

Vlad: Ah yes, I've been looking forward to this question. Now, before I get to my point, I want to make it clear what I am not saying here. I am not saying all other religions are wrong in every way, or that they have nothing to teach us, or that they are all going to hell, or that we shouldn't be open to interreligious dialogue. That is *not* what I am saying. All I am going to commit myself to here, is that when it comes to the nature of God, I think the Christian Trinity gets the closest to grasping who the divine is, and so that's how I can justify being a Christian instead of joining some other religion.

Idi: How correctly political of you.

Vlad: With that preamble in place, let me make my case. Now, we agreed there are three options for the origin of the universe?

Mira: Right. Being, Becoming, and Both. One of those has to be correct in some form or other.

Vlad: Right. So let's evaluate the God of Being, were the Being option alone to be correct.

Mira: So, like, if Being is correct, then what would God be like in that universe?

Vlad: Yes. I want to look at each option and see how it aligns with other religions.

Idi: Okey dokey.

Vlad: Now, if God is simply sheer Being, then could he create the universe?

Mira: No, because he can't *begin* to do anything, because to begin to do something requires Becoming, which is exactly what a God of Being lacks.

Vlad: So could he be called creator?

Mira: No.

Vlad: Now, could this God be called eternal?

Idi: Yes. He is utterly eternal. Unmovable, unchanging, static eternity.

Vlad: Yes, he is technically eternal, but his eternity is more of a prison than a privilege, for he cannot escape it in order to begin to create in time. What's more, wouldn't everything else also be eternal?

Mira: How so?

Vlad: Well, if Being alone is true, then there is no Becoming in the universe, thus all time, all change, all movement, is an illusion. Every moment of our lives has actually existed for eternity all along. Your dead mother is actually still alive in some other part of existence, and Elvis is still fat somewhere over the rainbow. God is eternal, yes, but so is everything else.

Mira: So if eternal Being is all there is . . . then . . . all there is must also be eternal?

Vlad: Exactly. God's eternity would no longer be his unique attribute but something that all creation—including humans—would share, for everything is eternal in a world where Being is all there is. So eternity no longer means what it used to mean, because it's not God's special attribute anymore but something he shares with everything.

Mira: It's like being the smart kid in high school, then going to Harvard and suddenly you're not the smart kid anymore. Sure, God would be eternal but everyone else would be as well, so it doesn't mean anything. Or at least, it doesn't mean as much as it used to.

Idi: *Augustus Gloop!* You sure came up with that Harvard example quickly. Are you dropping subtle character hints about your secret past? The plot thickens!

Mira: Your face thickens.

Idi: Your mom thickens.

Vlad: Now, if God is static Being, he is stuck in his inherent nature. He cannot begin to do or choose anything but is eternally stuck the way he is. He is more like a frozen statue then a personal being. Would you say that such a God is free?

Mira: No. At least, not free to do anything different than what he has been doing eternally.

Vlad: And could such a frozen God feel emotions, enter into the human experience, or relate to us in any temporal way?

Mira: Not that I can see.

Vlad: So is God in any sense personal?

Mira: Nope. God would have nothing to do with us at all.

Vlad: And could he reveal truths to us? Could God enter time and communicate with us in a way we could understand? Would God be *knowable*; knowable in the way that religions claim to know him? Or would his eternity be beyond our finite grasp, and so we could not say much about him at all?

Mira: Hmm. I guess he wouldn't be knowable in that case.

Vlad: So in sum, if only the Being option is correct, then God is neither truly free, creator, eternal, knowable, or personal.[32]

Idi: Ok. But what's your point? How does this relate to other religions?

Vlad: I'm getting to it. Be patient. Have I ever steered you wrong?

Idi: You don't want me to respond to that.

Vlad: I'd prefer if you didn't speak in general, actually.

Mira: I second the motion.

Vlad: So we've undermined a God of only Being. Such a God would not be truly free, creator, eternal, knowable, or personal. So any religion that wants God to have those attributes cannot be satisfied with just a God of Being. Now let's look at the God of only Becoming and see how he would fair.

Mira: Alright.

Vlad: So let us assume only the Becoming option is correct. Let us assume that the universe has existed for an infinite period of temporal Becoming. Would such a universe need a creator?

Mira: No, because it's always existed.

Vlad: And if the universe has always existed, then God's everlastingness isn't really something unique to him anymore, is it?

Mira: Hmm, I guess not.

Vlad: In which case, God is neither creator, nor is his everlasting and infinite nature a unique attribute of his divinity, because everything is infinite and everlasting.

Mira: Just like how divine eternity becomes meaningless if everything else is eternal as well?

Vlad: Exactly. God's unique status as everlasting and as creator are undermined. And if creation is just as infinite as God, then God doesn't really transcend the world anymore either. The creator is no longer an infinite being who transcends his finite creation, for now the universe itself is everlasting and uncreated. So, once you go with the infinite Becoming option, you really undermine the usual picture of God as transcendent, everlasting, or creator.

Idi: But what if the universe isn't infinite, but rather, the *cause* of the universe is infinite?

Mira: Wait, what?

Idi: On the Becoming option, we don't necessarily have to say the universe has existed for an infinite period of time, just that whatever caused it has existed for an infinite period of time. The causes have to stretch infinitely back, but the universe doesn't necessarily have to. So perhaps God existed for infinity, then later created the universe.

Mira: Oh, that's interesting.

Vlad: Ok Idi. I'll go ahead and address that. Now, in our previous discussion, we showed how all the parts of infinity are infinite. Remember the hotel with the infinite number of rooms? If half the hotel guests check out, there still has to be an infinite number of guests remaining (or else infinity would just be some finite number multiplied by two). Even if nine tenths of the guests check out, there would still be an infinite number of guests remaining. Which means that infinity requires greater and lesser infinites to exist.

Mira: Right, so, like, the nine tenths that checked out are a bigger infinite than the one tenth that remained, but both groups are still infinite.

Vlad: Exactly. Now, what this means is that the universe would have to be infinite no matter how long God waited before creating it. Even if God waited through nine tenths of his infinity before creating, that final tenth would still have to be infinite as well, thus rendering his creations infinite. A lesser infinite, but still infinite. On the Becoming option, it doesn't matter how small a part of infinity the universe has existed for, as all parts of infinity are infinite.

Idi: But why does that matter?

Vlad: Because then an everlasting life is not uniquely the property of God, but potentially belongs also to his creations.

Mira: So, again, just like how divine eternity becomes meaningless if everything else is eternal as well?

Vlad: Exactly.

Idi: Ok, yes, all things would be infinite, but God would still be the most infinite. He'd still be the biggest Kahuna.

Vlad: But then God is no longer qualitatively distinct from his creations, for both are infinite! You see, before, God could be infinite while the world was finite, and so there was a qualitative distinction. But once both are infinite, even if God is the bigger infinite, they become *qualitatively* on the same plane. God may be the bigger infinite—he may be *quantitatively* larger—but *qualitatively* they are both infinite in duration.

Mira: Ah, it's like my cats.

Idi: Your cats??

Mira: Yes. Mister Pudges is extremely fat. He weighs around 25 pounds, which is huge for a cat. He looks like a furry blowfish. Now, Mister Pudges always gets lots of love from guests because of his cuddly belly and how cute his chubby waddle is when he tries to walk. But recently I went out and got another cat, Roley Poley, who has now grown to 22 pounds.

Idi: What the hell are you doing to these cats?

Mira: That's not the point. The point is, Mister Pudges is no longer special anymore, and so has become jealous of the new cat. Everyone wants to rub Roley Poley's belly now too, because he also has lots of lovable blubber. *Yes he does.*

>*Idi rolls his eyes*

Mira: So even though Mister Pudges is actually three pounds fatter than Roley Poley, they are both still very fat, and so Mister Pudges is no longer unique. He may have more *quantity* of fatness, but *qualitatively* both cats are fat. In the same way, God may be the fattest among fat infinites in terms of quantity but he is no longer qualitatively distinct in a world where all is infinite Becoming. There is no longer anything that special about God's infinity.

Idi: Thank you for telling us about your cats. You've really added to the discussion.

Mira: Patronize much?

Idi: I am literally a patron in your bar.

Mira: Exactly. *My bar.* I could have you kicked out.

Vlad: Disbarred, as it were.

Idi: She doesn't have the balls.

Mira: You know, casual sexism can have just as many casualties.

>*Vlad laughs at the exchange.*

Vlad: That is one big pile of wit.

Mira: . . . So . . . getting back to my cats?

>*In the background, Idi begins to softly sing "Chubby Cat . . . Chubby Cat . . . what are they feeding you??"*

Vlad: Yes, Mira, your cats were a good illustration. In light of the aforementioned fat-cats, the doctrine of God existing forever would no longer have the same weight. Yes, God would still exist for infinity but created things could also exist for infinity—albeit a slightly less plump infinity.

So, could you say that God, on the Becoming option, is everlasting in any traditional sense?

Mira: No, not really. Or if he is, it only carries half the weight it had before. His everlastingness is no longer a distinct honor that belongs to him alone. Many created things could be infinite and everlasting as well.

Vlad: Precisely. And in the same way, if created things might be infinite, then does God's status as creator not seem a tad redundant as well? Sure, God would technically have created the universe an infinite period of time ago and would remain the bigger infinite. And yet if creation is still in some sense infinite, then it really feels like a creator becomes redundant. Why not just say creation is infinite on its own, and does not need a cause of its existence? God becomes a middleman, and those exist to be cut out.

Mira: So just like with God's eternity, God's status as creator would then lose its traditional weight? God may technically still be the creator, but not really in the way we usually mean.

Vlad: Exactly. So, this God of Becoming might be immanent with creation in a way the God of Being was not, but he would thereby forfeit any hint of transcendence. He may be infinite but so is creation. Such a God would just be an exaggerated version of created things, not truly transcendent or high enough to be worthy of worship.

Mira: Hmm.

Vlad: And another thing!

Idi: How many "thingies" are there going to be?

Vlad: Final thingy. If God is caught up in an infinite chain of causes, then each cause had a cause before it, and that cause had a cause, and so on and so forth. Thus, this God is caught in a deterministic chain. He is not truly free, for each of his actions were caused by a prior cause, and each of those causes had a cause, and so on and so forth, *ad infinitum.* A chain of Becoming—where each cause is said to have a cause—means there is no wiggle room. Thus, could this God be called free?

Mira: Certainly not. At least, not in the sense that we've been talking about.

Vlad: So to sum up, if the Becoming option alone is correct, then God is not free. God is also not transcendent, not creator, and not everlasting (at least, not in the usual or distinguished sense of those terms). Such a God would be no God at all.

Mira: Hmm.

Vlad: So neither the Becoming nor Being options allow any hint of a real God.

Mira: Which leaves the Both option?

Vlad: Which leaves the Both option, yes. Now, what does the Both option entail?

Mira: Both Being and Becoming. Both of them in one, paradoxical package.

Vlad: Right. And on this option, since God is Being, he can be eternal and transcendent. And since he is also Becoming, he can begin to create. He can thus be the creator of all. Further, in his Becoming he can also enter into our history, relate to humanity, communicate with us, whisper truths, disclose his nature. He can feel emotions in time, experience reality and humanity in a personal, empathetic, temporal way. Nietzsche said he would only believe in a God who could dance. Well this one can.

Mira: Hmm.

Vlad: As such, this God can be called personal and knowable. Furthermore, since such a God can act both within and beyond his eternal nature of Being, he has the recipe for freedom. Thus, this God can also be called free.

Mira: So the Both option allows God to be creator, eternal, transcendent, knowable, personal, and free all at once?

Vlad: Exactly. Everything that is wrong with Becoming on its own is cancelled out by the existence of Being, and everything wrong with Being on its own is cancelled out by the existence of Becoming. The Both option brings the two sides together to answer each other's problems. God has an inherent nature of eternal Being while simultaneously he is able to act beyond his inherent nature via his Becoming, allowing him to be free and personal. In his Being he can be eternal and transcendent, while in his Becoming he can be creator and knowable. Traditional theists as well as Christians must side with the Both option unless they are willing to sacrifice many of God's primary attributes.

Idi: So what's your point? How does this relate to my objection about other religions?

Vlad: Think about it. If God exists—at least the eternal, free, personal, creator God of the major monotheistic religions—then the Both option must be true. But if the Both option is true, then Being and Becoming are united in one seeming contradiction. They are not parts (e.g., 33 percent Being, 33 percent Becoming) for that would render it merely a combination and not a contradiction. For it to really seem like a contradiction, Being and Becoming have to exist fully in and of themselves, but also simultaneously as one. Thus, it must be 100 percent Being, 100 percent Becoming, and also 100 percent Both. Three and one. One and Three. So other religions have been inadvertently appealing to a Trinity all along, or at least, something shockingly similar. One plus one plus one equaling one is not the paradoxical embarrassment of our faith. Rather, it is the secret ingredient which other faiths have been unknowingly pining after and assuming.

Mira: Hmm.

Vlad: And all the other things that come with the Both option also follow. Without temporal Becoming, Being would be stuck in its atemporal nature. Thus, it can only be through Becoming *that all things were made*, and without Becoming *nothing was made that has been made*. Other religions must believe what John 1 has said all along, that all things were made through the second member of a Trinity. Though Becoming is temporal, in its inexplicable unity with Being it is also eternal. Therefore, created is inadequate to describe Becoming, for *there was never when it was not*; perhaps *eternally begotten* is more fitting. Which is exactly how Christians have described the Son for thousands of years.

Vlad takes a sip, then continues.

Vlad: And since Becoming is 100 percent its own individual and also 100 percent one with Being, it can simultaneously be said that at the creation of all things Becoming was *with* Being and Becoming *was* Being; *Becoming was with Being in the beginning.* Whereas atemporal Being is by definition outside of space and time, Becoming is temporal and so could possibly become *incarnate* and *make its dwelling amongst us* in the temporal realm. Though *no one could ever see Being*—for it is inherently beyond finite space and time—perhaps because Being and Becoming are one we could know Being through Becoming. Any other avenue to knowledge of Being is impossible for humans, for our temporal nature restricts us to this finite realm. Thus, *no one comes to Being except through Becoming.* No one comes to the Father except through the Son. The incarnation of Jesus is not the scandal of Christianity but the type of thing that is necessary for any religion that claims to have knowledge here and now of eternal truths.

> *Another pause. Another sip. Vlad takes a deep breath this time as well.*

Vlad: . . . As is hopefully becoming obvious, anyone who believes in an eternal, transcendent, personal, free, creator God, must inadvertently believe in something shockingly like the Christian Trinity. Now, I think this argues both for the uniqueness of Christianity and for its non-uniqueness. It is unique in that it grasps in *full* what other religions only see in *part*. But it is also that which is least unique for it is most general; it reveals itself as the secret lurking behind the attributes of all these other gods from the very beginning.

Mira: I've never thought of it that way.

Vlad: Though again, I definitely do not want to say all other religions are wrong about everything, I just want to explain why I am a Christian and not something else.

Idi: But your argument only addresses the big monotheistic religions like Judaism or Islam—religions that ascribe to one God who is eternal, creator, etc.,—but there are thousands of other religions in the world that don't fall prey to your critique because they don't need God to have all these attributes. Polytheistic religions or pantheistic religions, for a start.[33]

Mira: Yes, I think the other religions question is far too big to settle on one Christmas Eve in a pub. That would be absurdly arrogant. There's too much diversity, too much history, too much human experience for us to really generalize about other faiths so quickly and just dismiss them all at once.

Vlad: Well those are good points.

Idi: By the power of Grayskull! Does this mean I win?!

Mira: Not quite. It wouldn't be reasonable to expect Vlad to go through every single religion and debunk it case by case; that would never end, because new religions would pop up almost as fast as he could knock them down. Plus, it takes years to become enough of an expert in any religion to give a real analysis of it. But I would say Vlad's given as good an answer as anyone could reasonably expect, especially when it comes to dealing with the monotheistic faiths. I have never really thought of the Trinity that way. Never thought about how it can hold in place all this other stuff in religion. I think it's fair to move to the next objection.

Idi: Ha! You've got her on your side, I see. Whatever he's paying you I'll double it!

Mira: You're already paying double because you ordered twice as much alcohol as him.

Vlad: So, shall we enter the eighth objection?

Idi: Onward to the eighth objection!

Vlad: Which was?

Idi: Which was! . . . that, um—

Mira: —that God is a projection of humanity.

Idi: Yes. That's it! God is merely a projection of us. We take human attributes like love, power, or knowledge, multiply them by a bunch, then come up with the idea of an all-loving, all-powerful, all-knowing God. God is in *major* what we are in *minor*; he is merely a projection of ourselves, an imaginary friend we've projected onto the clouds, who merely repeats us and our ways of thinking back to us. The study of God is really just the study of humanity and our thoughts. So then we end up with what Feuerbach said: theology is anthropology.

Vlad: You were listening when I said it was Feuerbach, not Freud. I'm impressed.

Idi: I'm quite impressive, don't ya know?

Mira: You certainly make an *impression*, though what it is I dare not specify.

Vlad: So with question eight, I think we can only really answer it along with question nine. Do you remember what your ninth objection was?

Idi: Basically, how can finite beings speak of an infinite being?

Vlad: Right. How can we mortals speak of an immortal God, a God who is so "other," so heavenly, so perfect, so transcendent, that he is hardly graspable at all.

Mira: It's sort of like with aliens.

Idi: It is?

Mira: Ya, I mean, in our movies we always picture aliens the same way; like humans with a few tweaks. They still have a head, it's just bigger and more orb-like. We took humanity's prized possession of reason and the brain, and just sort of made it bigger in an alien. But any alien we'd encounter in reality wouldn't look like that. Aliens would probably have evolved so differently from us that we can't even imagine what they would look like.

Vlad: And that's like God?

Mira: Yes. I think so. Because even if there exists some supreme intelligence in the universe, he is probably so different from us that we can't even begin to describe him.

Vlad: Touché.

Mira smiles.

Vlad: Right. So, that is the ninth objection: how can we finite beings speak of an infinite Being like God? Now, if you notice, objection eight and nine are the exact opposite of each other. Eight says that God is just a projection of our humanity, while nine says that God must be so unlike humanity that we cannot talk about him at all. The first objection says he is too *like us* to be real, the second that he is too *unlike us* to be described using rational human language.

Idi: So as soon as you answer one side of the dilemma you inadvertently undermine the other. As soon as you make God like us then he becomes a projection of us. But as soon as you admit God is unlike us then he no longer fits into anything we finite humans with our finite language say about him.

Vlad: Perfecto! Now, what I want to propose is that the Both option answers this dilemma. Since God is Being, he is transcendent; above and beyond the realm of time and space. Yet since God is also Becoming, he can be known, reached out for, grasped using finite language. He is both like and unlike us, both subject and object, self and other, close and far, above and below, transcendent and immanent, mysterious yet knowable.

Mira: Right! Because you didn't reduce God to a projection of us, because your picture of God still defies our mental categories. . . . And yet . . . because you showed that it is still rational to believe in him you also didn't remove him from human discussion. You've . . . you've . . .

Vlad: Go on, Mira.

Mira: Well, you've . . . rationally justified the irrational. You've stepped out onto the slippery ice but haven't fallen through. Theology is not just anthropology because God does not fit into the categories and language of a finite human mind. Yet theology is also not just blind faith because you showed that it's as rational to talk about and believe in as our own existence.

Vlad: Exactly right, Mira, very good. I'm frankly shocked at your expertise, you really should be a professor.

Mira: Well, thank you.

Vlad: So the Trinity allows us to embrace both the distance and closeness of God; it is the bridge between us and eternity.

Mira: And so . . . so . . . that's why the incarnation is so important! Because it reveals in history what has always been true: that God is both like and unlike us.

Vlad: Right again! God is close enough to relate to us, connect with us, be understood and spoken about, just like Jesus in the incarnation. Yet far enough away to be more than a projection of us; to be transcendent and divine enough to be worth speaking about in the first place. God is somehow irrational enough to be beyond our human minds, yet rational enough for us to have a conversation about him. And this is where Jesus as the Logos comes in. In that chapter you quoted in the Gospel of John, it refers to Jesus over and over again as "the Word."

Mira: Oh good, I was wondering about that. Why is Jesus called that?

Vlad: Well, in Greek, the word for "word," is *logos*. Logos is connected with reason and thought. Logos is sort of like the rational structure that forms the universe and by which anything can be rationally known. It's where we get the term "logic" from. It's also where all these academic disciplines get the "ology" in the second half of their name from: geo-*logy*, socio-*logy*, anthropo-*logy*, psycho-*logy*, archaeo-*logy*, et al.

Mira: So, when the Bible calls Jesus the Logos, the Word, it implies that there is something rational about him?

Vlad: Exactly. It implies that Jesus, as the one through whom this world of Becoming was made, has created a world that is rational and imbued with the imprint of his divine Logos. Our world is rational, mathematical, *knowable*. We can study the disciplines—the "ologies"—and know reality through our reason, for reality was created by reason. By the logos.

Mira: Hmm.

Vlad: And yet, there is still something deeply mysterious about the universe, about God, and especially about the Father. Whereas the Son came as a man—someone we can see and touch and know in an intimate way—the Father of Being seems much too grand and mysterious for all that. The almighty, eternal Father rules from far away in the heavens and we cannot even see his face without dying, because he's just too bloody tremendous and transcendent for us to comprehend. Being is so absolute, so eternal, so Other, so beyond time and space that it seems like too much to grasp. And yet . . .

Vlad takes a deep breath, collecting his thoughts.

Vlad: And yet precisely because God is both the rational Logos of Becoming and the transcendent mystery of Being, he can be spoken of using rational argument and language without simply turning into a projection of human thought. It is only through the Logos that we can know the otherness of God. As we've paraphrased over and over, *no one comes to the Father except through the Son.*

Mira: And I guess that perfectly mirrors the whole system you've been setting out tonight. I feel rationally justified in embracing the irrational; your whole system tonight has showcased this very paradox of Jesus' Logos and the Father's transcendence. It's all so crazy, and yet it all feels so . . . so . . . reasonable!

Idi: Oh, I think reason left the building a long time ago now . . .

Vlad: Idi, if you can honestly claim that then you really haven't listened to what I've been saying or to anything I've ever said. I have no interest in abandoning reason for blind faith. In fact, many would say I am far too much of a rationalist; that I favor *logos* far too much over *pathos*. Since I was a boy, all I've ever done is question and think and probe the lackluster answers my teachers gave me. I *crave* answers. Cold, hard, objective answers, not sentiment. I love that I have been given a mind, and that so much of the world can be unveiled through thought. I have supped from the Logos as long and deeply as I can. And yet, it is precisely my desire to follow the evidence where it leads that has led me to this point. Logic has led me beyond itself; the Son has shown me the Father. And just when reason breaks down—just when it should all collapse into chaos—the Father points back to the Son in whom he is well pleased, and suddenly it all makes sense again. At least, as much sense as anything else.

Vlad: So let's move on to objection ten.

Idi: You're not even pausing to let me object anymore.

Vlad: Do you have an objection?

Idi: I could have an objection.

Vlad: But do you?

Idi: Of course I do.

Vlad: What is it then?

Idi: I'm formulating it.

Vlad: No you're not.

Idi: I could be formulating!

Mira: He's just trying to run down the clock.

Idi: Mwhaha.

Mira: Ten! Get to objection ten!

Vlad: So Idi said that absolute morality cannot possibly manifest in particular contexts, and so right and wrong have no objective meaning.

Idi: Ah, yes. The morality that works for one culture doesn't work for another. For example, in the West morality is all about the individual; about respecting personal freedom and consent and rights. But in the East, doing the right thing is more about family, community, tradition, honor.

Mira: Did you just generalize 7 billion people into two camps?

Idi: I've seen *The Last Samurai.* I know what I'm talking about.

> *Mira and Vlad roll their eyes in unison.*

Idi: What we deem good and what we deem evil are informed by our particular context. What we call right and wrong depends on where we live, on our culture, time period, race, religion—

Mira: —gender—

Idi: —age, experiences, genetics, and so on and so forth. There is not just one definition of "good" but a plurality of "goods." Instead of one meaning to the cosmos there is a diversity of meanings. Instead of a transcendent morality grounded in the nature of God we have context-bound moralities invented by the state.

Mira: So, because we all, like, exist in our particular contexts with our particular truths, there is no way to talk about one great big absolute truth for everyone and for always? . . . That's postmodernism, right?

Vlad: Well, postmodernism is one of those vague terms that's hard to—

Idi: —Ya, it's postmodernism.

Vlad: You know, Idi, to generalize all of postmodernism like that is precisely what "postmodernism" is fighting against.

Mira: How so?

Idi: Because instead of generalizing about reality, postmodernism wants to get knee deep in the particulars. People throughout history have always been trying to find one, unified, absolute truth that applies to everyone, everywhere, all the time. But what if reality cannot be generalized about like that? What if there is no abstract definition of what a "person" is, but just billions of individual people, each one so different and diverse that they cannot be understood in the abstract? What if there is no absolute definition of "right and wrong," but as many ethical systems and customs as there are cultures? What if there is not one true definition of who God is, but as many gods as there are religions? What if there is no deeper reality behind the diversity of the world; no deeper generalizations but just particular, local, individual, social customs? What if there is not one big *Truth* but just lots of little *truths*. That's what postmodernism is all about. But of course, as soon as you try to generalize what postmodernity is, you commit the very thing it's against.

Mira: Ok, well, embracing uniqueness and particularity . . . that doesn't sound so bad. Makes a lot of sense actually. I mean, it sounds like that helps us value unique individuals rather than just lumping everyone into one standardized box of what it means to be human. Like it helps us appreciate different places and times and cultures rather than just . . . just—

Idi: —just trying to colonize the world so everyone looks like a polite British gentleman?

Mira: Yes! A white, male, middle-class, allegedly heterosexual, British gentleman!

Vlad: And these are all great points. Postmodernism has much to offer.

Mira: . . . But?

Vlad: But what?

Mira: It sounded like a "but" was coming.

Vlad: Well a "but" was coming, but I didn't want to back it up too quickly. I didn't want to just negate the value of the postmodern. I think postmodernity really has something to say that we need to listen to.

Mira: . . . But?

Vlad: But, while it has a lot to say, it's not the whole story. See, if everything is particular and diverse and there are no higher truths, then what do you think happens to morality?

Mira: Well, it becomes customized to particular contexts. That makes sense to me, locals should get to decide what works best for their context. And precisely because they are contextual, they address the real concerns of those people rather than some abstract morality imposed from afar like English civility or American Capitalism.

Vlad: Yes, it is helpful if morality takes particular circumstances into account. But that cannot be *all* it does. Because if morality is just what one particular context says it is, then there is no higher morality by which that context can be judged.

Mira: Wait, what?

Vlad: Well, let's take criminals for example. If you listen to criminals and psychopaths talk in interviews, they don't always think of themselves as evil. In fact, they often may describe elaborate rules they follow. Things they will and won't do.

Idi: Criminals have their codes.

Vlad: Exactly. Now, if morality is entirely particular and there is no higher definition of right and wrong, then whatever morality a particular individual comes up with is perfectly valid. For there is nothing higher by which they can be judged. A criminal's code is as valid as any other.

Mira: Well of course I don't think every particular individual gets to decide for themselves what right and wrong are. That's why we have laws about these things. Society as a whole gets to decide what is right and wrong.

Vlad: Ok. So perhaps morality is not based on a particular *individual* but on particular *cultures*?

Mira: Yes. That's more like it.

Vlad: Ok. But if morality is just based on what a particular culture at a particular time says, then what about the slave trade?

Mira: Well, what about it?

Vlad: Well, for centuries slavery was considered moral by many cultures. And if morality is just whatever a particular time or culture says it is, then there is no higher standard by which that particular culture can be judged. Then you can no longer even say slavery was objectively wrong, because for that particular culture it was right.

Mira: Well of course the slave-driver nations thought it was ok, but the places that were being enslaved certainly did not! So it was never truly considered "moral" by everyone.

Vlad: But see, now you're trying to expand morality beyond particular contexts to find a more abstract definition of good. You're trying to find a definition of right and wrong that expands beyond what the slave-driver nations believed in order to encompass the views of the enslaved nations as well. You are moving beyond the definition of "good" in one particular place and trying to come up with an absolute "Good" that applies to *all* people and places.

Mira: Oh. I think I see that. Right and wrong cannot just be particular to one time or place. So, then, morality has to transcend time and place?

Vlad: Exactly. Morality has to be absolute.

Mira: What do you mean by absolute in this case though?

Vlad: Morality has to be engrained in absolute, eternal, Being.

Mira: Wait, we're back to Being again?

Vlad: Yes, we are. Because to be outside of particular times is to be timeless. Which was our definition of eternal Being.

Mira: Ah, yes, ok.

Vlad: You see, time and space constantly shift and change and evolve, and so any morality that is grounded in something within the shifting sands of Becoming will always be changing and evolving relative to particular contexts. But a morality grounded in something above and beyond time and space—a morality grounded in eternal Being—can provide an objective basis for morality. That way what is right is always right—eternally so—and doesn't change depending on whether the masses at any particular *time* decide that slavery is good or bad. It is in this sense that I say morality must be absolute. It cannot be grounded in the shifting sands of Becoming—in any particular time or place—but must instead be grounded in eternal, timeless, absolute, Being.

Mira: So, ok. I think I get it. Morality has to be absolute. But . . . we are all so . . . *different*. Our contexts and experiences and backgrounds are so very diverse. How can an absolute morality ever do justice to our particular circumstances?

Idi: Aaannnddd welcome to the problem.

Vlad: Yes, you've grasped the issue, Mira. We need to find a definition of morality that is absolute enough to transcend all times and places, and yet particular enough to somehow apply to those very same times and places. For we don't make ethical decisions in the abstract but in our lived contexts and daily routines; *moral conundrums always have flesh on their bones.* So how is it possible for an absolute morality of Being to enter into the particular Becoming of our unique times, places, cultures, classes, races, religions, genders, contexts, and experiences? Does this not seem like a contradiction?

Mira: Oh!

Vlad: Yes Mira?

Mira: I just . . . I think I know where you're going with this.

Idi: Well duh, he's going exactly where he's gone with every bloody thing tonight.

Vlad: Bingo! In the Trinity both absolute Being and particular Becoming are merged. Eternal truths are not negated by temporal circumstances, but can unite with, and incarnate within, them. The incarnation is the prime example, where moral perfection united with a particular time, place, culture, religion, and language. God enters into the particular context of the ancient Middle East, speaking the native language, learning the local customs, working within first-century mores, operating under the oppression of the Roman empire. Jesus is the image of moral perfection in time. In the incarnation, God reveals that he alone can bridge the gap between Being and Becoming, absolute and particular, noumena and phenomena, metaphysics and physics.

Mira: So, eternal Goodness, Truth, and Beauty can *incarnate* in particular cultures, times, and places?

Vlad: Yes. Just because anthropologists and sociologists can show that something is cultural doesn't mean eternity can't be woven into the cultural fabric. Particularity does not negate eternity. Becoming does not negate Being.

Mira: Hmm . . . You know . . . when I think about something that we do on earth that is somehow so much bigger than us . . . something in time that carries you out of time . . . I think of . . .

Idi: Go on, spit it out Lassie.

Mira: I guess I just imagine . . . that if our temporal universe had only one thing in it that was absolute . . . then it would probably have to be . . . love.

    Idi smirks.

Mira: Ok, I mean, yes, I know how that sounds and I'm sure how we show love and what we define as "loving" varies from culture to culture and what not. But still, underlying it all couldn't there be some core nugget of love that transcends cultures? We might all show it in different ways but there has got to be some common thing called love, right? I mean, doesn't the Bible say that "God is love"?[34] Makes sense to me that if God is love, and God is absolute, then love must be absolute. So . . . perhaps that's it! Perhaps when we love in our own particular ways and contexts we transcend to the absolute. Sort of like that line in *Les Mis*. To love, um . . . to . . . gosh, what is it?

Vlad: *To love another person is to see the face of God.*

Mira: Yes! To love another person—another particular person!—is to see the face of an absolute God. . . . Just as the personal is the mystery of the cosmos, so love is the mystery shared between persons! And doesn't that square perfectly with the whole Trinity thing? Each member of the Trinity loves the other members for all of eternity. But if God was just, like, one isolated entity on his own for all of eternity then there would be no one to love. So how could the Absolute be love unless the Absolute were in an eternal relationship? You cannot have love without lovers!

  Vlad puts his feet up on a nearby chair.

Vlad: She's making my case for me.

Vlad: I think that's about as close as we can get for now to answering the morality and meaning issue. How exactly all this looks in practice is a much bigger question, which, if answered fully, all the pubs in the world would not have enough room for the dialogues that would be written. But, at least, theoretically, we have shown that it makes as much sense as our own existence for an absolute morality or love to enter into our particular contexts.

Mira: So, then, you're not just using morality to prove the existence of God but the existence specifically of a *trinitarian* God?

Vlad: Hmm. Yes, to some extent it is an argument for the existence of the Trinity, isn't it? Objective morals cannot exist unless eternal Being can manifest in the realm of Becoming through some contradiction of Both, which is what believing in the Trinity allows. So morality points to the three and one and the three and one point back to and legitimate morality. Nihilism need not be the order of the day. Stop playing with fire Idi and go home to your family.

Idi: But there's still my other objections!

Vlad: Right. What was the eleventh complaint?

Mira: Diversity.

Idi: Ah, yes, *mein elf* objection! Religion is soooo intolerant of diversity. Christianity has historically been used to silence other ethnicities, other classes, other genders, other sexual preferences, other religions, other ideologies. All is sliced off once you get in to a procrustean bed with the church. God chews up all diversity and difference, vomiting back a smooth, homogenous malaise.

> *Mira frowns slightly, her eyes floating up and across the bar, settling on a nearby bottle of near-empty scotch.*

Vlad: Well, my friends, I think this question has already been answered, in a way.

> *Mira's eyes perk back up.*

Vlad: In fact, not only do I have an answer to why Christianity does not negate diversity, but why only the Trinity can possibly save diversity.

Idi: What?!

Mira: How?

Vlad: Look, I don't claim to be able to defend everything Christians have ever done throughout all of history. Obviously, we've done some horrible things in the name of God. Nor do I claim to have the answer to every squabble anyone's ever had with controversial Bible verses. However, . . . I do think that the Trinity is the only way to philosophically defend diversity.

Idi: Again, what?!

Vlad: You see, in order to defend diversity, you not only have to affirm the diversity we experience in the realm of Becoming, but you also have to affirm a moral absolute in the realm of Being, such that one could actually say that diversity *should* be morally encouraged.

> *Vlad leans back in his chair as if expecting applause. Upon receiving none, he frowns, then tries to articulate his point again.*

Vlad: You see, if absolute Being reigns on its own, it swallows up all uniqueness and diversity and particularity. For if at the heart of the universe everything is connected to some Absolute or a Platonic One then everything is swallowed up by that. Instead of billions of diverse humans, there is just one form of "humanness" that all persons must fit themselves into. Instead of particular cultures, ethnicities, etc., there is just *one* truth that supersedes and stifles the rest. All the uniqueness and particularity of Becoming is swallowed up in the one, homogenizing machine of the Absolute. All must be the same, for all must be absolute and one.

Mira: Yes I get that part.

Vlad: But then to avoid this our postmodern culture swung too far in the opposite direction. We rejected the one and embraced the many. We rejected all unity and emphasized diversity; all of us are unique, all of us are different, and there is no overarching form of "humanness." No absolute norms.

Mira: But that's not totally a bad thing though . . .

Vlad: To some extent, it's not. We should be open, respectful, tolerant, and loving to those who are not like us. But if you take the particular and the many too far, you end up negating all meaning and morality in the universe.

Mira: How so?

Idi: Because.

> *They both turn to look at Idi.*

Idi: Because then all norms, all morality, all standards are shed. There is no right or wrong, because everyone is just different. The criminal, the deviant, the selfish; they are not wrong, but just different ways of doing things. There is no higher unity, no underlying way to behave. You can't even say love is inherently good, because the unloving person could just say they are different and unique. There are no higher absolutes; everything is just particular and relative. A world without unity, without any absolutes, without Being, without any norms . . . that would be a *meaningless* world.

Mira: So . . . this is why for you, Idi, if these objections weren't answered it wasn't just your faith that was over but, well, everything? I heard you say this earlier, but I guess I'm only just now getting what you meant on a gut level. You're worried that if there is no higher meaning then morality, love, family, . . . all of it . . . is a cruel illusion?

Idi looks away and nods.

Vlad: Yes Mira. That is correct. For if you over-emphasize the particular realm of Becoming then you end up with nihilism; you end up emphasizing difference to the point that there is no common unified truth, not even love or goodness. You can't even say we *ought* to be tolerant of diversity or accepting of people who are different, because there is no "ought," there is no morally right way we all ought to behave. So in trying to make diversity good you've inadvertently abandoned the idea of "goodness" itself, and so lost any moral basis for why we *ought* to tolerate or encourage diversity in the first place. . . . But, on the opposite end, if you overemphasize absolute Being you swallow up all individuality and particularity. And so once again, diversity is lost.

Vlad wipes his brow before continuing.

Vlad: Now most worldviews jump back and forth between these two extreme's when it's convenient, without really developing a coherent worldview. But the enigma of the Trinity allows us to keep the proper tension. Since God is *both* one *and* many—indeed, one and three—he enables us to wed the absolute and particular, unity and diversity, Being and Becoming. Only a trinitarian worldview can hold Being and Becoming together, legitimating the realm of diverse Becoming while also providing a moral foundation in Being for why tolerance of diversity is morally "good" to begin with.

Mira: And so, even if Christians have done some cruel things to shut down diversity in the past, you can at least say that only a trinitarian view of the universe can actually legitimate diversity in the first place?

Vlad: Exactly. Only if someone assumes a trinitarian worldview can they even really critique the mistakes of Christian history to begin with. Otherwise, they have no philosophical foundation to defend diversity, and are left ricocheting back and forth between Being and Becoming with no way to bridge the tension.

Mira: Hmm. I'll have to think about this some more.

Vlad: While you do that, let me complicate matters by toying with another idea. You see, it's not just that the Trinity provides an absolute basis for us to say that tolerance of diversity is ethically good. No, it's more than that. For *the Trinity is itself unity-in-diversity; three persons unified as one God.* Though the persons of the Trinity are different, they are nonetheless united as one; identity-in-difference. So diversity is not some later aberration or deviation or invention but is rather baked into the nature of things from the very start.

Mira: Wait, what?

Vlad: See, if at the heart of existence there was just one thing, then diversity would somehow be a later perversion of that original unity. In turn, if at the heart of existence there were many things, then there would be no underlying unity to existence, and so all would be a postmodern chaos, with no unifying truths, morals, or meaning. But the Trinity allows there to be both unity and diversity at the heart of everything; three diverse persons, yet one unified God. Without the Trinity the universe would ultimately reduce to either a fundamental unity or a fundamental diversity, but the Trinity allows *both* to co-exist together. Unity-in-diversity. One and many. Three and one.

Mira: Oh, ok I guess that makes sense. So . . . that's it then? You've really done it!? You've used the Trinity to answer all the other big questions!

Vlad: Yes. The Trinity is the linchpin for everything else. Without the mystery of the Trinity at the center of all things, all else becomes mysterious. It is the light that one cannot look at, but in light of which all else is seen.

Mira: Then the debate is over!

Idi: Not quite. You are forgetting the final objection! Your front line of defense—the Father, Son, and Holy Ghost—remain shockingly male. How do you explain this eternal misogyny, this bearded father in the clouds, this phallic shadow cast upon creation?

VI

THE THREE AND ONE

Idi: Why is the Trinity, the central thesis of your whole rant, so callously sexist? You've been referring to God as "him" the whole night!

Mira: Ya, it's always upset me that there is a Father and Son but no mother.

Vlad: Well, I can't claim to answer it once and for all, but I do have a couple of thoughts, if you'll permit me.

Idi: You've only got about fifteen minutes until the pub closes. I'm gonna win . . .

Vlad: I'm going! Well, first of all, our previous discussion transitions perfectly into this one. For as I just argued, it is only because of the Trinity's ability to hold together the moral unity of Being with the diversity of Becoming that I can rationally affirm diversity in the first place. So if I am angry that there is no gender diversity in the Trinity, it is only on the basis of the Trinity that I can even legitimately defend that anger to begin with.

Idi: Fine. But you're really milking that point.

Vlad: Then let us move from milk to solid food. Now, in the Bible, the term used for "Spirit" is often feminine. Many ancient languages—and some modern languages—give words a gender; male, female, or neuter.

Idi: The literal basis for "neutered."

Vlad: In the Hebrew Bible, and in the original Aramaic that Jesus spoke, Spirit is feminine. In light of this, some Christians consider the Holy Spirit the female component of God; the divine mother. In fact, you might have noticed that I keep referring to the Spirit as "it." This isn't because I think the Spirit is an object or thing, but because I'm not entirely sure whether to call "it" a *he* or a *she*, or something beyond even those categories.

Mira: I didn't know that about the Spirit in the Bible. Why don't people talk about that more?

Vlad: Well, the fact that the term "spirit" can be feminine doesn't automatically prove that the Spirit itself is feminine. Even inanimate objects can have gendered language; that doesn't prove that a teacup is female.

Vlad pauses for a second, musing.

Vlad: Though I suppose that's not the real reason a lot of people reject it. Some are just more comfortable sticking with the bearded father in the clouds.

Mira: That's interesting. . . . I guess I've always felt the exact opposite way. I've never felt comfortable with God as Father. My father wasn't exactly the sweetest man. But my mother, now she was a different story. I could see the divine in her all along.

Vlad: Indeed, there are even some Bible verses that talk about how we can know the nature of God through our mothers. Psalm 22 says, "you took me from the womb; you made me trust you at my mother's breast" (Ps 22:9).

Mira: Hmm.

Vlad: In fact, one of the names Christians use in relation to God is "Sophia," or the female personification of holy wisdom.

Mira: As in, *Hagia Sophia*, that famous cathedral in Constantinople?

Idi: Istanbul.

Vlad: Yes, as in *Hagia Sophia*. Good connection, Mira.

Mira: Thanks.

Vlad: What's more, there are Scripture verses where God is referred to with feminine imagery. God is described as a mother in Hosea, Deuteronomy, Isaiah, and, I think, in the Psalms too.

Idi: A couple of random verses isn't really enough though . . .

Vlad: Well, the kicker is in the very beginning, in the book of Genesis, when God first created humanity. It says God created them in "God's own image: male and female." So both men and women are made in the image of God. Again, the image of God is similar to how a child is made in the image of their parents, looking and talking and acting like them. So to say that the image of God is both male and female means there's got to be something feminine in God that is uniquely represented by human females that cannot be captured by anything else.

Mira: Hmm.

Vlad: What is more, "traditional" masculinity isn't exactly associated with intimacy and relationality. And yet, the Trinity says that instead of some isolated, rationalistic, lone-ranger substance at the heart of the universe, there is rather a relationship. A relationship so intimate that the walls between the ones held in its embrace begin to blur; three and one, one and three. As Jesus says: "I and the Father are one." Of course, I don't want to say intimacy is inherently feminine, but you can see how this relational God does not exactly fit into traditional views of lone-ranger masculinity either. There is something else going on here.

Mira: So . . . God is a woman?

Vlad: Well, no, I wouldn't go that far. I don't think God has genitalia or a sex in the same way humans do.[35]

    Mira nods in agreement.

Vlad: See, I think the primary point of the Father, Son, and Spirit is not that God is male or female. But rather, that the intimacy of the family construct is a reflection of just how intimate the divine relationship is. And since the family structure is what the Trinity plays off of, motherhood is always implicit in family imagery of the Trinity, even if making that explicit wasn't the most effective way of communicating God to a deeply patriarchal culture.

Mira: What do you mean by "communicating God"?

Vlad: I just mean that if you wanted to start a religion in the Middle East two thousand years ago, there was simply no way anyone was going to listen if Jesus was female. Now, Jesus radically elevated the status and treatment of women, but he was only able to do that and have others follow suit because he was a man. So, is God literally male, or was that just the most effective way to *communicate* to a male-dominated culture?

Mira: That makes sense. Plus, I suppose adding another mother to the family imagery of the Gospels would have been a bit redundant, as Jesus already had a human mother.

Vlad: Yes, there already is a mighty mother in this Christmas story; Mary, the mother of God. As Saint Augustine said: "He whom the heavens could not contain the womb of one woman bore. She ruled our ruler, she gave milk to our bread; she carried him in whom we are."

Idi: *Orc Mischief!* Are you worshipping Mary now?

Vlad: Not at all, I'm just agreeing with Mira that the family imagery of the Gospels would have been redundant if there were two mothers in the narrative.

Idi: I could have done with two mothers, considering my dad.

Idi forces a chuckle, then looks away.

Vlad: I know Idi . . . I know.

A pregnant pause follows.

Mira: . . . I wonder though . . . if perhaps God came to us as a loving Father, precisely because he knew there would be such a lack of them?[36]

Vlad: I've answered all your objections, Idi. You have much to go home for, much to go on for, much to preach in the name of!

Idi: Boooo! I don't think you've answered anything. This is all nonsense!

Vlad: Of course it's nonsense! But it's nonsense that maps onto our nonsensical cosmos. Reason oversteps when it begins to make more sense than reality.

Idi: But you've just made matters even more mysterious than they were before!

Vlad: Yes, I have spread mystery, but I've justified the spread of mystery. That was my whole point about connecting the origin of the universe with the Trinity!

Idi: I'm still not sure if it works or not though.

Vlad: Ah, but see, you and I are both biased. Mira should decide who won between us.

Idi: Fine. So what will it be Mira? Is Christmas a crock or not? Should I go home or stay out on the prowl for lonely lovers?

Mira: I need a minute. I have to think.

Vlad: Take your time. Someone's future hangs in the balance.

Idi: She's stalling.

Mira: No, I'm not.

Idi: Yes, you are.

Mira: No, I'm really not.

Idi: Um, yes, you really are.

Mira: Shut up.

Idi: Ok.

Mira: Really? It's been that easy to shut you up the whole time?

Idi: Well, I am you.

Vlad: True. We are one.

>   *All three of them nod in perfect unison.*

Mira: Don't break character!

Idi: Sorry. Actually, I'm not sorry, because I'm not allowed to talk.

Mira: You can talk. Just be good.

Idi: Freedom!!!!

Vlad: You're drunk, Idi.

Idi: Yes, I am. But only because you are. And no thanks to Mira, who is the worst bartender ever.

Mira: Technically, I'm a professor, not a bartender.

Vlad: Being a professor explains why she's been able to sit here and chat with herself the last hour while she's supposed to be serving other customers.

Idi: Yes, and why she had so many brilliant insights.

Mira: Quit spelling out the plot! . . . Wait, you think I'm . . . brilliant?

Idi: I think I'm brilliant. If that logically entails your brilliance, then that is a sacrifice I am willing to make.

Vlad: I think this whole drunk arguing is good for us. It allows us to have the debates we wouldn't be comfortable having when we're sober. It's good to be open and honest with yourself.

Idi: Lame.

Vlad: I'm just doing my job.

Idi: Yes, but you don't have to be such a square about it.

Vlad: Well, how should I go about soul-ing?

Idi: You're just trying way too hard. It's annoying.

Vlad: As opposed to you?

Idi: Um, yes! You don't see me putting up a fuss. I'm just enjoying life.

Mira: Yah, because it's *soooo* hard to be our body; eating, drinking, shagging, pooping. You've really got a full schedule.

Idi: Hey! I am a finely tuned machine. Have you seen my glutes?

Vlad: Yes, but for all your exercise you have almost no self-control.

Idi: The body wants what it wants. You see that guy in the corner? You could grate cheese on those abs! Go fetch!

Mira: But . . . you've been flirting with me the whole night!?

Idi: Yes.

Mira: But how does that make sense if you're also me?

Idi: I'm your body . . . and you're lonely . . .

Mira: So?

Idi: Search your feelings Mira, you know it to be true.

Mira: . . . Oh.

Idi: Mwhaha—

> *Idi's crude laughter turns into another coughing fit.*

Vlad: Idi was not always like this, Mira.

Idi: Like what? What was I not always like? *Do tell the tale of me.*

Vlad: Idi was once a body that was tender, tamed, fierce, and passionate; a strong mare. But now Idi's become a bad joke, driven on by every passing whim, by every fleeting temptation of the flesh. Weariness, work, and lack of affection has made our body a hollow reflection of its true self, a withered skeleton of its former strength and potential.

Idi: Well, tell me what you really think.

> *Idi clutches his chest in mock offense.*

Vlad: Let us waste no more time on this. The decision is yours, Mira.

Mira: I don't think I can. It's all just way too much.

Vlad: I know it's hard, Mira, but time is running out. The sun will soon rise on Christmas morning. You need to help us come together to make this decision.

Idi: Yes, without you we'll get nowhere. What would Vladimira be without Mira? We'd just be Vladi. And who the hell is called Vladi? No one, that's who. . . . Though I suppose no one is really called Vladimira either.

> *Idi sighs.*

Idi: Father is to blame, really. No shock there. . . . Bastard wanted a boy named Vladimir, and when a girl popped out he just added an "a" at the end. . . . For the life of me, I never knew why he—

Vlad: —Ok, now you're just self-disclosing to wind down the clock.

Idi: *Clever girl.*

Mira: Why it is that even when I'm just talking to myself I picture two dudes? Women have been so brainwashed by our misogynistic culture that we even man-splain to ourselves!

Vlad: And tell yourselves the same degrading things you hear from the outside world. Idi is simply a projection of how we think about ourselves every single day.

Idi: You are nothing more than meat, Mira, nothing but *carne*, flesh, womb and warmth! Let's stay out tonight, find some random guy, and let him have his way with us.

Mira: And what is the soul's council?

Vlad: That the body is good . . . *but that doesn't mean everything we do with it is.* Let's go home to our husband and kids. At least for tonight.

Idi: If they could give us what we need then why are we even here having this conversation to begin with?

Mira: It's not like that. Things have just been so . . . *overwhelming.* At work, at home. Everyone wants everything from me, and I don't know how much I have left to give.

Vlad: Yes Mira, we are burning the candle at both ends for everyone else. And we have needs of our own as well; physical needs, emotional needs, existential needs. But tonight is not the night to meet them; not half drunk on Christmas Eve with some guy in a pub. You are searching for eternity in all the wrong places. Let's go home. Sleep. Eat some turkey. Then let's talk again when you are thinking straight.

Mira: I understand what I should do. . . . But I've just had all these doubts that have been plaguing me for years, you know? Doubts about God. Church. Faith. Love. The Universe. Free will. Morality. Meaning. All of it really. . . . And I thought that was the real issue with why I've been struggling. But now that I've answered some of those question, I'm still just . . . just—

Vlad: —just right back where you started? Having chased all the rabbit trails of the mind, it all comes back to an act of will. A choice. A decision to either do the right thing or not.

Mira: Ya. . . . And I just don't trust myself to make that choice. I don't have it in me.

Idi: You don't. *You really don't.*

Vlad: I promise, Mira. I promise that you do.

Mira: How do you know?

Vlad: For while you often choose the things that harm you and those you love, I swear that this is not your truest nature. You're fashioned out of ancient cloth, woven in the image of time beyond time. You, O woman, are made in God's own image, and that same love between the Three— that love that spawned our cosmic cradle—is felt by them for you. What is more, a fire a billion years of age now rages on beneath your breast, stoked by the One who is Three, whose act of creation replays itself each day in you. The paradox that birthed a thousand worlds now dwells within, and you can wield it freely for the good. You, O daughter of God, are so much more than this temptation, so much more than this moment in time. Rise. *Get up.*

> *With these final words, Vladimira is left sitting on her own in the pub, snow streaming against the windows in silence, and the pages of Hume's* Dialogues concerning Natural Religion *splayed open in front of her. She pauses there for a while, eyes darting back and forth between the front door and the moderately attractive gentleman in the corner. Suddenly, she shuts the book, slaps two bills on the counter and rises hurriedly from her seat. Staring straight ahead, she marches determinedly toward the exit, not straying to the left or right. But as her hand clutches the doorknob, she pauses, then turns back and whispers to herself.*

Vladimira: But what about the priests and those little boys?

Endnotes

1. This is somewhat similar to the argument Alvin Plantinga made in *God and Other Minds*. His work first evaluates the traditional arguments for and against the existence of God, finding neither side compelling. Plantinga then evaluates the arguments for and against the existence of other minds, discovering the same epistemic stalemate that was present in the theistic question. This parallel launches his peculiar thesis that belief in God is much like belief in other minds. Neither can be proven or disproven convincingly, but since this epistemic ambiguity does not render belief in other minds irrational, neither should it render theism irrational. If belief in other minds is rational, so is my belief in God. But obviously the former is rational; so, therefore, is the latter. This does not blindly justify belief in anything and everything, however (Santa Claus, dragons, astrology, etc.), for the parallel to other minds is only applicable when no valid counterarguments exist and there is a *prima facie* case to believe in each. For example, there are legitimate queries regarding Santa's existence, such as How can he get around the world in one night? or How can he eat all those cookies and still fit down the chimney? My argument, though vastly different in content, as well as dealing with explicability rather than epistemic justification, is of the same broader type as Plantinga's.

2. Muir, *Variations on a Time Theme*, viii.

3. This is, of course, a reference to Hilbert's Hotel. See Hilbert, *David Hilbert's Lectures on the Foundations of Arithmetic and Logic*.

4. Craig makes a helpful comment about this, remarking that once the logical leap from finite to infinite is made things can indeed work coherently within that paradigm, but that the issue is the initial leap itself: "The late Oxford University philosopher J. L. Mackie disputed [these objections to the infinite] because the so-called absurdities of the existence of an actual infinite are resolved once we understand that for infinite groups Euclid's axiom 'The whole is greater than its part' does not hold as it does for finite groups. Similarly, Quentin Smith comments that once we understand that an infinite set has a proper subset that has the same number of members as the set itself, then the purportedly absurd situations become perfectly believable. *But far from being the solution, this is precisely the problem. Because in infinite set theory this axiom is denied, one winds up with all sorts of absurdities such as Hilbert's Hotel when one tries to translate that theory into reality. The issue is not whether these consequences would result if an actual infinite were to exist; we agree that they would. The question is whether such consequences are metaphysically possible.* That question is not resolved by reiterating that they would

be possible if an actual infinite could exist. Moreover, not all the absurdities result from a denial of Euclid's axiom: The absurdities illustrated by guests checking out of Hilbert's Hotel result from subtraction of infinite quantities, which set theory must prohibit to maintain logical consistency." William Lane Craig, *Time and Eternity*, 225. Italics added.

5. Or, as Russell puts it in regards to God: "If everything must have a cause, then God must have a cause. If there can be anything without a cause, it may just as well be the world as God, so that there cannot be any validity in that argument. It is exactly of the same nature as the Hindu's view, that the world rested upon an elephant and the elephant rested upon a tortoise; and when they said, 'How about the tortoise?' the Indian said, 'Suppose we change the subject.'" See Russell, *Why I Am Not a Christian*, 3–4.

6. Some interpretations of "eternity" are that it is not "outside of" time but is rather an everlasting time. This is obviously not how I am using it, and such a view would, I believe, simply manifest the issues of infinity, for eternity in this case would then mean an infinite, everlasting time. As such, this view of eternity is dealt with and encompassed by the previous section.

7. ". . . for us physicists believe the separation between past, present, and future is only an illusion, although a convincing one." Letter of Albert Einstein, March 21, 1955, quoted in Hoffmann and Dukas, *Albert Einstein, Creator and Rebel*, 258.

8. The same point could be made regarding metric conventionalism. Even if the Oxford School, a group of scholars that includes Richard Swinburne, Alan Padgett, and John Lucas, can successfully strip time of any intrinsic measure, it still would seem to violate our mind's temporal categories through which we view the world, for the mind phenomenologically seems to present us with a world that does in fact have an intrinsic measure. Thus, it defies one of the fundamental lenses through which we view reality, which is all I need to prove for my argument.

9. One might retort that analogy could mystically combine like and unlike, and so if the steps between Being and Becoming are ontologically analogous steps then this crossing of the qualitative chasm may be possible. Now, if analogy merely combines like and unlike parts in a mixture (e.g., 55 percent of one, 45 percent of the other) than this mixture is reducible back into univocal and equivocal parts, and so doesn't really accomplish the goal of analogy. However, perhaps analogy does not just crudely mix distinguishable parts (e.g., like oil and water) but creates some mystical union of the two entities that cannot be rationally reduced to separate parts. But this is actually quite close to what I will ultimately propose: that the relation of Being and Becoming defies—or is "above"— rational analysis. Thus, I do not claim analogy is false but simply that it does not make complete sense to our finite minds (which is all my argument needs to show and which many of its proponents would readily admit).

10. One might wish to argue that there is a fourth option: A, non-A, both A and non-A, *and neither A nor non-A*. However, this gets too far beyond our purview here, and indeed, if the binary of time/timelessness were somehow transcended, this would likely require something beyond our cognitive lens of temporality. If something like that is possible, it would at least be beyond our mental lens of time, and so fit into my broader argument about the origins of the universe not making sense to our finite minds.

11. All biblical quotes are taken from the New International Version, 1984.

12. One could argue that a contradiction does not avoid heresy but rather both does

and does not commit heresy, at the same way and in the same time. Thus, while it would be 100 percent orthodox, it would also be 100 percent heretical, for Jesus would be 100 percent not eternal. A good response to this comes from Jc Beall: "[heresies] need to be understood in a way compatible with the possibility of Contradictory Christology. In particular, a familiar heresy concerning Christ's divinity may be understood in at least two ways: H1. Presence of Negation: the theory contains the given negation (viz., 'It's false that Christ is divine'). H2. Absence of Nullation: the theory fails to contain the given 'nullation' (viz., 'It is true that Christ is divine'). The current objection charges that Contradictory Christology, as advanced here, commits a heresy in the H1 sense; but there is no suggestion that the theory commits a heresy in the H2 sense. By my lights, it would not be surprising were the truth of Christ, who is the unique contradictory being at the center of Christian theology, to involve 'heresies' in the H1 sense. After all, that Christ exemplifies two complementary natures (the joint satisfaction of which entails a contradiction) may bring about falsity claims that appear to be deeply heretical (i.e., H1–heretical); but the substantial heresies, at least by my lights, involve an outright rejection of the orthodox claims—the absence of such claims from our Christology. The substance of serious heresy is in H2: namely, having a theory that rejects or omits the given truth (e.g., that Christ is divine, that Christ is human, etc.)." Jc Beall, "Christ—A Contradiction, "424.

13. For example, William Lane Craig, previously argued that thoughts involve temporal processes, and so there would have been temporality in the divine mind prior to creation itself (though this seems to differ from his current view of divine timelessness prior to creation). Craig, ed., *Time and the Metaphysics of Relativity*, 191–92; *God, Time, and Eternity*, 14, 194.

14. You might be worried that a contradiction annihilates any difference between the Father and Son. Yet the exact opposite is arguably true. For while logic forces us to choose whether they are one or many, a contradiction allows that they could simultaneously be both. It is the law of non-contradiction that forces us to choose between identity and difference.

15. Gunton writes that the "Spirit has to do with the crossing of boundaries. Spirit relates to one another beings and realms that are opposed or separate. That which is or has spirit is able to be open to that which is other than itself to move into relation with the other. It is particularly but not only used of God and the world. By his Spirit God comes into relationship with the world, creating and renewing, as in Ezekiel's vision of the valley of the bones, in Luke's story of the new act of creation whereby the child is formed in the womb of Mary, and in the resurrection of Jesus Christ from the dead. The result of this movement is that by his Spirit God enables the creation to be open to him. In the Old Testament, the word *ruach* founds a way of speaking of human empowerment and so is relational and particularizing. 'Most of the texts that deal with the *ruach* of God or man show God and man's dynamic relationship. That a man as [*ruach*] is living, desires the good and acts as authorized being—none of this proceeds from man himself.' A similar relational way of speaking is to be found in some New Testament characterizations of the work of the Spirit (When we cry Abba! Father bearing witness with our spirit, Romans 8.15–16). Spirit thus brings God into relation to the world and, reciprocally, the world into relation with God. But it is not only a matter of God and the world: it has to do with human spirit, too. Paul's saying that he is absent in body but present in spirit is a way of suggesting that created beings may in a limited way

transcend the space to which they are tied. That, then, is the first aspect of what it means to be or have spirit: it is to do with the crossing of boundaries, with opening out of people and things to one another. The second feature is that the Spirit, far from abolishing, rather maintains and even strengthens particularity. It is not a spirit of merging or assimilation of homogenization but of relation in otherness, a relation which does not subvert but establishes the other in its true reality. This is especially evident in biblical characterizations of the work of the divine Spirit, the perfecting cause of the creation. It is in terms of particularities that we can understand many of the ways in which the New Testament characterizes the relation of Jesus and the Spirit. . . . A similar function can be seen to be performed by the Spirit in the ministry of the church after the ascension, when, according to the theology of the Fourth Gospel, the Spirit takes up the work of Jesus by relating particular believers to the Father through him. The Acts of the Apostles is full of instances of how one course rather than another was chosen under the impact of the Spirit's guidance. Another focus is provided by Paul's conception of the Spirit of the Lord as the giver of human freedom. According to this conception, the freedom of Christians derives from their institution a new particular network of relationships: first with God through faith in Christ, and then with others in the community of the church. Just as the Spirit frees Jesus to be himself, so it is with those who are in Christ, that is, in the community of his people. The church is a community, not a collective: that is, a particular community into which particular people are initiated by the leading of the Spirit. It follows that . . . the Spirit respects the otherness and so particularity of those whom he elects. That is why Paul's characterization of the various charismata, in I Corinthians 12, for example, is so seminal for our conception of what it is to be in community, for it implies richness and variety, not homogeneity. It is here that we find the nub of the difference between the gospel and the modern world. God the Spirit is the source of autonomy, not homogeneity, because by his action human beings are constituted in their uniqueness and particular networks of relationality. It is by virtue of both of those features, the crossing of the boundaries and the preservation of particularity, that I would argue that the notion of spirit is so important for our understanding of ourselves and our world." Gunton, *The One, the Three, and the Many*, 181–84.

16. The analogy of a child need not imply that the Spirit is the Godhead's child. For in the family construct it is not merely the children that are derived from two, but the parents themselves who also exist as the cumulative product of their own parents. The point is not that children are one-from-two, but that all humans are one-from-two. Thus, what is applicable to the Spirit need not be the family construct of a child, but the cumulative nature of personhood itself. All persons are unions, not just those who happen to currently be young. One need not carry the image further than that, for it is the very nature of an analogy that it is not exhaustive.

17. "As part of nature, *pneuma* . . . is both material and spiritual, both natural and divine, . . . it is never wholly outside the realm of sense. Whether in terms of Aristotelian noeticism, modern idealism, or the NT understanding, it is never set in antithesis to matter. . . . For when the author, who stands in the Jewish tradition, wants to speak of the work of the *pneuma*, he has to bear witness to the immaterial God on the one side and yet also declare on the other that this God has acted and still acts concretely in matter. The *pneuma* shares both God's transcendence over the world and also his participation in the events of this world . . . ." Kittel, *Theological Dictionary of the New Testament Vol. VI*, 335, 358, 373.

18. "The *locus classicus* of its [the law of non-contradiction's] defense is Aristotle's *Metaphysics*. It is a striking fact about the Law that there has not been a sustained defense of it *since* Aristotle (at least, that I am aware of). Were his arguments so good that they settled the matter? Hardly. There are about seven or eight arguments in the chapter (it depends how you count). The first occupies half the chapter. It is long, convoluted, and tortured. It is not at all clear *how* it is supposed to work, let alone *that* it works. The other arguments in the chapter are short, often little more than throw-away remarks, and are at best, dubious. Indeed, most of them are clearly aimed at attacking the view that *all* contradictions are true (or even that someone can *believe* that all contradictions are true). Aristotle, in fact, slides back and forth between 'all' and 'some,' with gay abandon. His defense of the LNC is therefore of little help." Priest, Beall, and Armour-Garb, eds., *The Law of Non-Contradiction*, 29.

19. Kant distinguished between the analytic and synthetic a priori, for he considered the law of non-contradiction to be more fundamental than causality, temporality, or spatiality. However, as will be borne out through the rest of the argument in this section, this preference for logic is unwarranted, for: "Kant nowhere gives an even moderately satisfactory theoretical account of the dichotomy between analytic and synthetic a priori propositions; nor can any be gleaned from his casually scattered examples. Among propositions generally counted as a priori there are, of course many distinguishable subclasses and in the history of controversy concerning such propositions, many philosophers have followed Kant at least to the extent of wishing to restrict the title analytic to the members of one or more of these subclasses. But it is very doubtful indeed whether any clearly presentable general restriction of this kind would release into a contrasted class of synthetic a priori propositions just those types of proposition which Kant's epitomizing question was meant to be about." Strawson, *The Bounds of Sense*, 33.

20. Perhaps numbers or abstract ideas might provide the mind with a thought that transcends space or arguably even time. Yet there are multiple arguments for and against this, and the broader discussion has a much longer history than we can do justice to here.

21. "Have you ever talked to a flat-earther, or someone with really bizarre religious beliefs—not one who subscribes to such a view in a thoughtless way, but someone who has considered the issue very carefully? If you have, then you will know that it is virtually impossible to show their view to be wrong by finding a knock-down objection. If one points out to the flat-earther that we have sailed round the earth, they will say that one has, in fact, only traversed a circle on a flat surface. If one points out that we have been into space and seen the earth to be round, they will reply that it only *appears* round, and that light, up there, does not move in straight lines, or that the whole space-flight story is a CIA put-up, etc. In a word, their views are perfectly consistent. This does not stop them being irrational, however. How to diagnose their irrationality is a nice point, but I think that one may put it down to a constant invoking of ad hoc hypotheses. Whenever one thinks one has a flat-earther in a corner, new claims are pulled in, apparently from nowhere, just to get them out of trouble. What this illustrates is that there are criteria for rationality other than consistency, and that some of these are even more powerful than consistency. The point is, in fact, a familiar one from the philosophy of science. There are many features of belief that are rational virtues, such as simplicity, problem-solving ability, non-adhocness, fruitfulness, and, let us grant, consistency. However, these criteria are all independent, and may even be orthogonal, pulling in opposite directions. Now

what should one do if, for a certain belief, all the criteria pull towards acceptance, except consistency—which pulls the other way? It may be silly to be a democrat about this, and simply count the number of criteria on each side; but it seems natural to suppose that the combined force of the other criteria may trump inconsistency. In such a case, then, it is rational to have an inconsistent belief . . ." Priest, *The Law of Non-Contradiction*, 32.

22. Perhaps the ground-consequent relation is distinct from the cause-effect relation, but they still have to coincide at some point, for while a belief may not get its epistemic validity solely from a cause, the occurrence of the belief in our mind at all must have some cause in order to occur in the first place. Further, there must be some cause within humans that causes some people to pursue solid thinking while others do not, or else the difference between idiots and geniuses is causeless. The same argument can be made with other species, for if the ground-consequent relation were somehow self-evident without need of some cause to acknowledge the validity of rational claims, then why are humans and gnats and sloths not equally knowledgeable, for our mental hardware should have no causal relation to what belief's we come to.

23. Now, is this a contradiction or just a physical impossibility? This is a difficult question. For could any physical reality be conceived or created where two opposite things exist in the same place at the same time and in the same way? Certainly, no such reality can be pictured, for this verges on square-triangle territory. Now, one might point to something like neutrinos, which fly through the earth at the speed of light. Yet neutrinos can do this because they fly through the empty space in matter, not because they co-exist with other matter at the same time in the same place in the same way. One might retort by pointing to fields, which co-exist with the particles within them. However, fields may exist at the same time and in the same place as particles, but certainly not *in the same way*. Fields are (arguably) somewhat ontologically unique from the particles that exist within them, and so are not as extreme an example as the atoms of a face and the atoms of a fist co-existing in the exact same place, at the same time, *in the same material way*. (In more logical terms: A and non-A, Face and non-Face, would have to be true at the same time, in the same place, in the same way.) Now, even if the physical nature of things could have been different, nonetheless, once that nature is established, there seems to be the possibility of contradictions within it, where the established nature of a face contradicts the established nature of a fist. And even if our example could not truly rise to the status of a logical contradiction, it still seems to be as nearly close to one as you can get within our physical and contingent world, leading to similar results of practical absurdity.

24. In case you are wondering: If the Son is Becoming but cannot have a beginning in time then do all the problems of a universe without a beginning apply to him (i.e., all those arguments about the incoherence of an actual infinity of past events)? The answer would have to be yes if we were trying to be logical about things. Because then we would have to find a way to logically resolve eternity and temporality, and the way to do that is in infinity (i.e., something that always exists but does so in time). But if we refuse to logically resolve them, then Jesus is simultaneously both outside of time and inside of time, and so is timelessly eternal (i.e., not infinite) but also contradictorily able to act in time. Of course, the mind attempts to resolve this into a picture or rational idea, in which case it ends up sounding phenomenologically a lot like an infinite, but the point is that this rational resolving is a mistake, for the reality is not rational (or at least, does not need to seem to us to be rational).

25. "Our differing attitudes toward past and future events serve to underline how deeply ingrained and how strongly held our tensed beliefs are. If the static theory of time is correct, feelings of relief, nostalgia, dread, and anticipation are all irrational. Since such feelings are ineradicable, the static theory would condemn us all to irrationality. In the absence of any defeater for our belief in the objective distinction between past, present, and future, such a belief remains properly basic and the feelings they evoke entirely appropriate. . . . Think, for example, of the difference in one's attitude toward birth and one's death. On the static theory of time the period of personal non-existence which lies after one's death is of no more significance than the period of personal non-existence which lies before one's birth. And yet we celebrate birthdays whereas we typically dread dying, a dread that runs so deep that one's death, wholly in contrast to one's birth, seems to put a question mark behind the value of life itself. Many existentialist philosophers have said that life becomes absurd in light of my death; but no one has said this with regard to my birth. [And] phenomenological analyses of temporal consciousness have emphasized the centrality of past, present, and future to our experience of time. In his classic analysis of temporal consciousness, the great phenomenologist Edmund Husserl described our experience of time in terms of remembering the past and anticipating the future, both anchored in consciousness of the now. The transformation of a now consciousness to a past-consciousness and its replacement by a new now consciousness, says Husserl, is part of the essence of time consciousness. Similarly, the psychologist William Friedman, who has made a career of the study of our consciousness of time, reports that the division between past, present, and future so deeply permeates our experience that it is hard to imagine its absence. He says that we have an irresistible tendency to believe in a present. Most of us find quite startling the claim of some physicists and philosophers that the present has no special status in the physical world, that there is only a sequence of times, that the past, present, and future are only distinguishable in human consciousness." Craig, *Time and Eternity*, 130–39.

26. Though his broader argument is drastically different from my own, William Lane Craig—channeling Al-Ghazali—also notes this parallel between a free act and the origins of the universe, for only a free entity could choose to begin to create in time. Craig, *The Kalam Cosmological Argument*, 151.

27. One might be wondering if the Son of Becoming somehow represents the indeterministic or uncaused side of things, and, if so, is he without an inherent nature? In response, I'd agree that the parallel is not really between Becoming and indeterminism. It's not that the Son of Becoming is uncaused, out of nothing, or some sort of "non-nature" (for indeed, in the realm of Becoming things have causes; real deterministic causes in time and space. Becoming itself has a nature.) Yet when Being and Becoming meet there is this odd phenomenon where something is created that wasn't dictated by the nature of Being nor by the nature of an infinite series of deterministic causes in Becoming, but by the union between them. Though it is an act in Becoming you cannot say it is caused by an infinite regress of Becoming because it originates in Being. But nor can you say that it is caused by Being, for Being alone cannot begin to cause anything. And so something new has begun in time that is caused neither by eternal Being nor an infinite regress of Becoming, and so is in some sense uncaused. (But of course, contradictorily also caused.) Just as the bearpig cannot be reduced to its parts, so too the resulting choice cannot be reduced to 50 percent Being nor 50 percent Becoming, and so is something genuinely new. So it is not that Becoming itself is a "non-nature" but

that when Being and Becoming come together something appears to arise from their union that is uncaused (i.e., not explanatorily reducible to its causal parts). The second half of the parallel is thus not really between indeterminism and Becoming, but between indeterminism and the *union* of Being and Becoming.

28. Now, it would be easy to call this third, mediating connection our spirit. As we've already established, the Greek word for spirit (*pneuma*) is both eternal and temporal, bodily and immaterial. And in the Bible *pneuma* is something that both God and humans have. There is the Holy *Pneuma*—the Holy Spirit—and the human *pneuma*—the human spirit. However, I have no need to pin down my view of free will to a specific tripartite view of the terms body, soul, and spirit. The biblical writers would often use terms like soul and spirit interchangeably while at other times distinguishing them. As such, it is hard to make any real doctrine of those terms based on sheer exegesis. By creating the dichotomy between the body as the changing finite and the spirit and soul as engaging something less temporal (Matt 10:28; Luke 8:55; Acts 7:59; 1 Cor 5:3–5; 1 Thess 5:23), they have led my initial dichotomy between body and something deeper, which is often called soul. But as for what the mediating entity between the body and soul should be called, I wouldn't want to stretch exegesis too far. I am making more of a philosophical point rather than an exegetical one.

29. The same response could also be given for why the body is a genuine and affirmable part of human identity. For even though the body may be changing, it is not exterior to our deeper self, for it is paradoxically one with our soul. Thus, even though there is a spiritual self that continues beyond the particular instantiations of body, body is still not secondary to selfhood but is always bound up in our identity through its paradoxical union with soul (in the same way that soul may be unchanging and yet can somehow change through its union with the body). Again, this makes as much (or little) sense as the existence of the universe.

30. Or perhaps the body is the determinative aspect and the soul is that which rises above and beyond it, and the two are united in the spirit. Indeed, there are many different ways to imagine this configuration. The point is not really the details of how it works out but the possibility that it somehow could, and that this would make as much sense as our own existence.

31. As stated earlier, a contradiction cannot be reduced into a logical mixture of parts, and so the free acts that are created by this union are not reducible to the nature of the soul nor to our circumstances in the body but are genuinely new and free.

32. Furthermore, the idea that God and creation tenselessly co-exist seems to negate God's triumph over evil. On the static theory of time, evil is never really vanquished from the world: "It exists just as sturdily as ever at its various locations in space-time, even if those locations are all earlier than some point in cosmic time (for example, Judgment Day). Creation is never really purged of evil on this view; at most it can be said that evil only infects those parts of creation which are earlier than certain other events. But the stain is indelible. What this implies for events such as the crucifixion and resurrection of Christ is very troubling. In a sense Christ hangs permanently on the cross, for the dreadful events of A.D. 30 never fade away or transpire. The victory of the resurrection becomes a hollow triumph, for the spatio-temporal parts of Jesus that were crucified and buried remain dying and dead and are never raised to new life. It is unclear how we can say with Paul, Death is swallowed up in victory! (1 Cor. 15:54) when, on a static

theory of time, death is never really done away with." Craig, *Time and Eternity*, 214.

33. Indeed, a number of Eastern (or even New Age) movements might choose to take the contradiction of Being and Becoming away from God's internal relations and relocate it to God's relationship with the world, making Divine being one with all created becoming, and arguing that this is as rational as our own existence. While this is not necessitated by my argument (as shown in my response to pantheism in chapter 3) it is still perhaps a possibility opened up by it. I note it here, though my proper engagement with this question will need to wait for a future book.

34. This helps remind us that morality is not an additional absurdity which would multiply absurdities beyond reason. For the eternal standard of goodness and love is not something that exists *in addition to* God, but rather, God *is* Love. God *is* Goodness.

35. This is not meant to be edgy. Indeed, historical Christian orthodoxy has always insisted that God is not literally male (even while it debated whether God has masculine qualities). As Robin Parry writes: "The first issue to be clear about is this—God is not male. Indeed Christian orthodoxy has always emphatically denied that God is male. God is not male; God is not female; God is not a blend of both. God transcends sexuality. So language about God as 'the Father' and as 'the Son' was always understood, when applied to God, in such a way as to strip away the literal male dimension of it. This much is undisputed." Parry, *Worshipping Trinity*, 189.

36. I've heard versions of this phrase before but have been unable to track down its source.

Appendix A

At one point during the evening's conversation, Vlad argued that if the cause was eternal the effect must be eternal as well, which is why a timeless Being could not begin to create in time (at least, not without contradicting). In an alternate universe, this conversation briefly split off on a side tangent, with Idi insisting that God could timelessly will to create time, and that this involved no contradiction. Using a quantum spanner, we have accessed a transcript from this alternate timeline.

Vlad: So, once again, temporal Becoming cannot arise from Being. Being and Becoming are opposites; one is outside of time the other is inside of time. No matter how cleverly you try and mix them they always contradict. God cannot *begin* to create time.

Idi: I think you're missing the point. Theologians do not think that God changes or suddenly *begins* to create. No, he timelessly creates time. He eternally wills to create a universe that isn't eternal. Creation did not begin *in* time but is the beginning of time itself. You cannot ask what God was doing before he created time, because words like *before* and *after* only make sense once you have time. So from God's perspective he eternally wills to create, and from our perspective the universe begins when time begins. But those two perspectives don't contradict because they don't exist on the same continuum. Eternity cannot be mapped as before or after on the horizontal line of time. Rather, God's eternity is on a totally different axis. Here, it's like this:

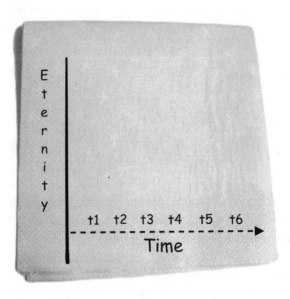

Idi: See, creation does not start at a moment in God's time such that we can ask why he began creating at point t rather than t+1 or t+2. For there is no time prior to creation. And so God's eternity exists on a different level or plane or axis. You can't ask what God was doing *before* he created time, because there is no *before* and *after* until time already exists. God timelessly wills to create time, and those two perspectives don't contradict because they don't exist on the same continuum. Time is chugging along horizontally, but God's eternity is vertical.

Mira: Wait, what? But . . . isn't that just restating the problem? I mean, of course you can't ask what existed *before* time, but that's Vlad's whole point. Time needs to already exist in order to explain how it could *begin* to exist. And so appealing to something outside of time in order to explain the beginning of time solves nothing.

Idi: I feel like you're not even listening to me.

Vlad: Idi, I understand what you mean about time and eternity not existing on the same axis or plane. But there has to be some relation or place where they overlap, or else how can you even say that Being *caused* Becoming? Even on your chart they have to come together in at least one spot. At 0. The x and y axis inevitably overlap.

Vlad circles the spot on the napkin.

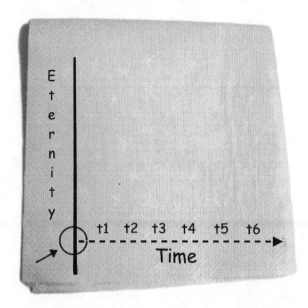

Vlad: And that's the point. If Being creates Becoming, then somewhere—however tiny, however brief—eternity and time have to meet. But that relation—that momentary interaction at year 0, that tiny place where the x and y axis overlap, where time arises from eternity—that is what we don't understand. That which is in time is opposite from that which is timeless; contradictions inevitably result from any attempt to bring them together, however brief.

Mira: Yes, exactly!

Vlad: Now, Idi, if you just want to say it's a mystery, then ok. I can respect that. Perhaps eternity exists on a totally different plane and is beyond the limited understanding that we have as beings within time. Perhaps as soon as we ask what is *before* time we have already projected our finite and temporal categories onto that which is supposed to be outside of time. Perhaps we should just admit that our finite, temporal minds simply cannot understand that which is beyond time, so perhaps Being can create Becoming in some magical way we just don't have the capacity to grasp. But note that you would have then admitted my bigger point: that we can't rationally understand how the universe began. Which is all I have been trying to prove this entire time.

Bibliography

Beall, Jc. "Christ—A Contradiction: A Defense of Contradictory Christology." *Journal of Analytic Theology* 7.1 (2019) 400–433.

Craig, William Lane. *God, Time, and Eternity: The Coherence of Theism II: Eternity.* Dordrecht: Kluwer Academic, 2001.

——. *The Kalam Cosmological Argument.* New York: Barnes and Noble, 1979.

——. *Time and Eternity: Exploring God's Relationship to Time.* Wheaton, IL: Crossway, 2001.

——, ed. *Time and the Metaphysics of Relativity.* Philosophical Studies Series, vol. 84. Dordrecht: Kluwer Academic, 2001.

Doyle, Arthur Conan. *The Sign of the Four.* Reprint, Garden City, NY: Doubleday, 1977.

Fraenkel, Abraham Adolf, Yehoshua Bar-Hillel, and Azriel Lévy. *Foundations of Set Theory.* 2nd rev. ed. Studies in Logic and the Foundations of Mathematics, vol. 67. Amsterdam: Noord-Hollandsche U.M., 1973.

Gunton, Colin E. *The One, the Three, and the Many: God, Creation, and the Culture of Modernity.* Cambridge: Cambridge University Press, 1993.

Hilbert, David. *David Hilbert's Lectures on the Foundations of Arithmetic and Logic, 1917–1933.* New York: Springer, 2013.

Hoffmann, Banesh, and Helen Dukas. *Albert Einstein, Creator and Rebel.* New York: New American Library, 1983.

Kittel, Gerhard. *Theological Dictionary of the New Testament,* vol. VI. Reprint, Grand Rapids: Eerdmans, 2006.

Lennon, John, and Yoko Ono. "Imagine." *Imagine.* Recorded May–July 1971. Produced by John Lennon, Yoko Ono, and Phil Spector. Vinyl, 1971.

Muir, Edwin. *Variations on a Time Theme.* London: Dent, 1934.

Parry, Robin A. *Worshipping Trinity: Coming Back to the Heart of Worship.* 2nd ed. Eugene, OR: Cascade, 2012.

Plantinga, Alvin. *God and Other Minds: A Study of the Rational Justification of Belief in God.* Ithaca, NY: Cornell University Press, 1990.

Priest, Graham, J. C. Beall, and Bradley P. Armour-Garb, eds. *The Law of Non-Contradiction: New Philosophical Essays.* New York: Clarendon, 2004.

Russell, Bertrand. *Why I Am Not a Christian, and Other Essays on Religion and Related Subjects.* Reprint, New York: Touchstone, 1982.

Strawson, Peter Frederick. *The Bounds of Sense: An Essay on Kant's Critique of Pure Reason.* Reprint, London: Routledge, 1995.

What if God is as rational as our own existence? Sitting in a pub one Christmas Eve two friends hash out their doubts and questions about God, the Trinity, and existence itself. They agree that the Christian Trinity does not make much sense, yet when they look at the origins of the universe, they realize it also does not make sense, and for exactly the same reasons. And if the enigma of the Trinity is the same one underlying the universe, then perhaps the Trinity is as rational to believe in as our own existence. Yet as the night goes on, they realize the same tact can be taken with lots of other mysteries as well, including free will, the soul, God, eternity, truth, and meaning. If such things were not real, then would we even exist to talk about it?

"You could buy this book on the merits of the subtitle alone! It sets the tone for the tome: apologetic integrity cloaked in irreverent honesty. It reads like the *Screwtape Letters* baptized in the blood of Captain Jack Sparrow. This is a rare jewel that will make you laugh as hard as it will make you think."
—**MARK MOORE,** author of *Core 52*

"Jonathan Lyonhart has produced an entertaining and vivid guide to the central Christian doctrine of the Triune God. He has truly succeeded in rendering its more technical aspects accessible to the ordinary reader without surrendering its inaccessible mystery and its invitation to wonder."
—**JOHN MILBANK,** University of Nottingham

"Five parts Socrates to three parts David Hume to two parts *Calvin & Hobbes*, Lyonhart provides ordinary lay readers with a disarmingly sophisticated account of the Trinity, the church, free will, faith, morality, love, and, as Douglas Adams might have put it, "life, the universe, and everything." *MonoThreeism* may well be absurdly arrogant, but it is also enormously useful, as well as being a good deal of fun. I can hardly wait to recommend it to my students."
—**CRAIG GAY,** author of *Modern Technology and the Human Future*

"*MonoThreeism* is magic, quite literally. I don't know how Lyonhart does it, but he's managed to pack ten books' worth of wicked wit and mesmerizing wisdom into a single and wonderfully readable book. . . . An eccentric masterpiece."
—**T. W. S. HUNT,** author of *Way of Faith* and *Winter with God*

"While the Dialogue has traditionally enjoyed an eminent role in the history of philosophy, it has sadly fallen into desuetude of late. Jonathan Lyonhart has remedied this in a book that employs wit, verve, and intellectual brio in a vigorous exploration of the doctrine of the Divine Trinity. Strongly recommended!"
—**DOUGLAS HEDLEY,** University of Cambridge

J D Lyonhart is an assistant professor of Theology and Philosophy at Lincoln Chri
University and a Fellow at the Cambridge Centre for the Study of Platonism. jdlyonhart.c

I S B N 978-1-7252-6268

COVER DESIGN: Mike Surber
www.wipfandstock.com

Cascade Books
An Imprint of WIPF and STOCK Publishers